Gender Equality and Genocide Prevention in Africa

This book investigates what impact gender equality has on genocide in Africa, to verify whether it is a missing indicator from current risk assessments and models for genocide prevention.

Examining whether States characterized by lower levels of gender equality are more likely to experience genocide, Timmoneri adds gender indicators to the existing early warning assessment for the prevention of genocide. Moreover, the book argues for the formulation of policies directed at the improvement of gender equality not just as a means to improve women's conditions but as a tool to reduce the risk of genocide and mass atrocities. Using case studies from Nigeria, Ethiopia, Angola, Uganda, and Burundi, Timmoneri analyses recent atrocities and explores the role of gender equality as an indicator of potential genocide.

Gender Equality and Genocide Prevention in Africa will be of interest to students and scholars of political science, genocide studies, and gender studies.

Serena Timmoneri holds a PhD in Political Sciences from the University of Catania.

Gender Equality and Genocide Prevention in Africa

The Responsibility to Protect

Serena Timmoneri

Routledge
Taylor & Francis Group

LONDON AND NEW YORK

First published 2019 by Routledge

2 Park Square, Milton Park, Abingdon, Oxon, OX14 4RN
605 Third Avenue, New York, NY 10017

Routledge is an imprint of the Taylor & Francis Group, an informa business

First issued in paperback 2020

British Library Cataloguing-in-Publication Data
A catalogue record for this book is available from the British Library

Library of Congress Cataloging-in-Publication Data
A catalog record for this book has been requested

ISBN: 978-0-367-07590-3 (hbk)
ISBN: 978-0-367-78810-0 (pbk)

Typeset in Times New Roman
by Apex CoVantage, LLC

Contents

5 Conclusions 85

Tables

Introduction

During the 1990s, the international community witnessed an array of humanitarian crises. Although at that time international law already proscribed specific kinds of State behaviours within national borders, genocide, ethnic cleansing, mass atrocities, and mass internal displacement of citizens were still happening. As a result, in 1999 Kofi Annan challenged the international community to develop a way of reconciling the twin principles of sovereignty and the protection of fundamental human rights. In 2001 the International Commission on Intervention and State Sovereignty (ICISS) provided a report on the new concept of the so-called 'Responsibility to Protect' (R2P), which was based on the 'responsible sovereignty' principle. This norm entailed a shift from the idea of 'sovereignty as control' to the concept of 'sovereignty as responsibility'. The protection of people's most fundamental rights from egregious violations became the underlying reason for sovereignty. This notion overcame the Westphalian concept of sovereignty based on the 'non-interference' principle, conceived primarily as the right to act within national borders without being internationally accountable. Although national governments are responsible for their citizens, when a State is unwilling or unable to protect its own people from gross violations of human rights, the responsibility shifts to the international community.

R2P imposes a responsibility on States not to harm and to pro-actively protect their populations, along with placing a responsibility on the wider international community to engage in an appropriately authorized and multilateral action (including, when needed, coercive force) to protect those populations if the particular States involved cannot or will not fulfil their responsibility. R2P is conceived around three key points: prevention, reaction, and rebuilding. Over time its structure has changed; however, the basis of the norm remains. Today, R2P is built on three pillars and military intervention has lost much of its centrality. The R2P report identifies prevention as the single most important dimension of the R2P doctrine and states that the prevention option should always be exhausted before forceful military action is contemplated. It is both politically and normatively desirable to act to prevent mass atrocity crimes from being committed rather than to react after they are already underway. In fact, among other things, good prevention allows the world to avoid one of the most controversial matters in international relations: the unending tension between the protection of individuals from the systematic violation of human rights and the protection of State sovereignty by external interference. However, atrocity prevention requires tailored engagement because the relationship between armed conflict and mass atrocities is highly complex and not well understood. In fact, despite that strong correlation between the two phenomena implies a direct link, not all conflicts give rise to mass atrocities and many atrocities occur in the absence of armed struggle. Therefore, it is not to assume that efforts to prevent or resolve conflicts will always simultaneously reduce the likelihood of mass atrocity crimes, including genocide. In addition, while an appreciation of particular regional and local dynamics is critical, many of the most promising preventive tools such as finding or monitoring missions, satellite surveillance, mediation, targeted sanctions, or no-fly zones require already existing structures, skills, and technology if they are to be applied in a timely and effective fashion. Moreover, existing early warning mechanisms to prevent mass atrocities are almost totally gender-blind. It means that they do not recognize any distinction between the sexes and incorporate biases in favour of existing gender relations, resulting in a tendency to exclude women. These mechanisms do not recognize that women and men are constrained in different and often unequal ways and therefore may have different needs, interests, and priorities. Thus, for as accurate as they are, risk assessment and models for genocide prevention are not perfectly accurate yet.

Prevention of genocide is still partial and some indicators are still missing. This research seeks to discover what impact gender equality has on genocide and to verify whether it might be one of these missing indicators. Indeed, many scholars have argued that a domestic environment of gender inequality and violence results in greater likelihood of violence both at the national and international level. According to the existing literature, there is a correlation between levels of violence, international conflicts, intra-state armed conflicts, civil wars, and gender inequality. Societies that are more equitable are supposed to be more peaceful because women have a say over matters of war and peace and they are generally more averse to war than men are. Alternatively, societies that are more equitable may be more peaceful because the norms of inviolability and respect that define equal relations between women and men are carried over to wider relations in society. This project aims to upgrade this line of inquiry. This research seeks to discover what impact gender equality has on genocide. The main hypothesis is that the lower the gender equality, the greater the likelihood that a State will experience genocide. The aim of this project is to test whether States characterized by lower levels of gender equality are more likely to experience genocide. In the first chapter of the book, I introduce the theoretical framework of my research, starting from the 'Cooperation Paradigm' and describe how and why the international community gave birth to the R2P norm. I analyse this norm in detail focusing in particular on prevention and early warning. After that, I make an excursus on the presence/absence of 'gender' in R2P developments and of gender-sensitive early warning mechanisms. Finally, I present the importance of adding gender-sensitive indicators in early warning frameworks for genocide prevention concerning R2P. In the second chapter, I present the literature on the correlation between gender equality and violence. I explain how gender equality and violence might be correlated, presenting the theory of structural violence (Galtung, 1975), showing how other scholars used it to prove the correlation between gender equality and violence and how it fits well for genocide. Finally, I present the literature on genocide, its different definitions, and the existing preventing models.

In the third chapter of the book, I present the case studies (Nigeria, Ethiopia, Burundi, Angola, and Uganda). After a general introduction on every country, I analyse the gender equality of every country in detail.

Finally, in Chapter 4, I present in detail the limitations of the study, the data, and methodology I used. Then, I compare the Country Risks of Genocide and Politicide Index Score of Barbara Harff and Ted Gurr with the data of Genocide Watch; using statistical analysis, I measure the influence of gender equality on the eruption of genocide, and finally I present the results of the research.

Beyond theoretical inquiry, I calculate the covariance, the standard deviation for gender equality and genocide, and the Bravais-Pearson correlation coefficient to test the preceding hypothesis, taking Nigeria, Ethiopia, Angola, Burundi, and Uganda in 2009 as case studies. This research analyses the overall gender equality in these five countries through the data of the Global Gender Gap (GGG) Report 2009 of the World Economic Forum and through the OECD's (Organization for Economic Cooperation and Development) Social Institutions and Gender Index (SIGI). Starting from Harff and Gurr's Country Risks of Genocide and Politicide Index Score (2009), I use gender equality to try to understand why, with similar scores, some countries experienced genocide while others did not. The main goal is to test whether there is a correlation between gender equality and genocide, in order to start considering the addition of gender indicators in the genocide prevention models and early warning mechanisms concerning the R2P.

The presence/absence of genocide is tested with Genocide Alert from Gregory Stanton's Genocide Watch. The research shows that Ethiopia (where the genocide was already underway in 2009) gets the same score (in Harff and Gurr's Risk Index Score) as Angola where, according to Genocide Watch, the level of violence did not turn into genocidal violence after 2009. Moreover, Nigeria (the only country that experienced genocide after 2009) gets the lowest score among the five case studies. Thus, to the usual considered variables calculated in Harff and Gurr's Risk Index Score, I added an analysis on gender equality in the case studies to measure the 'weight' that gender equality had on the eruption of genocidal violence, using the data elaborated by the Global Gender Gap Report of the World Economic Forum.

The hypothesis of the research is confirmed. There is a moderate correlation between gender equality and genocide. Consequently, a way to tailor the efforts in order to improve prevention of genocide and mass atrocities might be to take in consideration gender equality. As previously observed, we cannot rely on generalized models of mass atrocity prevention; thus we need to elaborate an apparatus that engages with 'real-time' developments all over the world. It is here sustained that adding gender indicators to existing risk-assessing models of genocide prevention might help enlarge perspectives on prevention of genocides. It might generate a greater commitment to improve gender equality as one of the means to reduce the risk of mass atrocities concerning the R2P (which is almost totally gender-blind), since the negative repercussions that lower levels of gender equality have at the societal level go beyond the negative impact on women.

The innovative character of this research is the proposal to add gender indicators to the existing early warning assessment for the prevention of genocide and the proposal of formulating policies directed to improve gender equality not just as means to better women's life conditions but as a tool to reduce the risk of genocide and mass atrocities.

1 Engendering genocide prevention

1.1 Cooperation in a world of conflict

Scholars see politics as a series of interactions focusing on either cooperation or conflict. Cooperation is based on transaction, exchange, and negotiation to formulate different positions on the use of shared goods while conflicting interactions are based on antagonism between incompatible ideologies and values concerning the use of assets of the system. For the 'conflict paradigm',[1] the aim is to pursue and exercise institutional power that gives the beneficiary the ability to use the goods and to regulate the system's processes to its advantage, while for the 'cooperative paradigm' the aim of politics is to maintain a distributive order with consensual practices. In the cooperative paradigm, political institutions are primarily instruments for social integration and unification, while in the conflict one they are coercive instruments. In the analysis of international politics these approaches are known as the Hobbesian (conflict) and Groatian (cooperation) paradigms, and many scholars (Belligni, 1991; Bartelson, 1996) have written about their differences. This research is placed in the context of the cooperation paradigm. The paradigm of cooperation was formed by Grotius and Pufendorf in the same period as that of conflict and inequality. According to this paradigm, relations between States are not only guided by different national interests but also by shared social and moral principles.

For Grotius, the identity of States as actors, which are social by nature and tied to moral obligations towards the society of which they are part, is the basis of the society of States. Nevertheless, the international political system is not marked by stability and harmony based on the equal sovereignty of its members, because States pursue contrasting interests. This can give rise to violations of the rules and attempts at their reformulation or even subversion. In addition, the emergence of the diversity of collective actors in competition with the States contributes to the volatility of the organization of the international system. The pluralist concept of 'world society' takes into consideration the tendencies to diminish the exclusive role of States as political actors and managers of the world's resources. According to this conception, international relations can no longer be reduced to the single dimension of the State because activities beyond government control have become relevant and are exercised beyond State borders by non-State actors. Unlike States, these actors are not characterized by the control of territory and people by a sovereign authority endowed with coercive means, but they do give rise to a global political system characterized by 'politics of groups' (Attinà, 2011). All manner of actors are able to influence binding collective decisions and these are reached through an *ad hoc* negotiating process. According to Bull (1977), the basis of international order is to be funded in international society through the set of relations between States and defined by elementary rules of coexistence (i.e. respect of undertakings, limitation of physical violence, and conservation of the property), rather than in the international political system (i.e. the totality of international relations determined by the most powerful States). These societal rules, which produce an international order, aim at guaranteeing the preservation of the diversity of independent and sovereign States, and also contribute to the formation of the international political system because they are part of the political institutions created by the States. Given the interaction between the social order and the political sphere, the international political system rests on three factors:

- the common will and interest of States to respect the fundamental characteristics of social life and the survival of States as sovereign and equal actors;
- the rules of coexistence (i.e. the respect of agreements and of property, and the limitation of physical violence) which proscribe behaviours necessary for the maintenance of social life;
- political institutions (i.e. international law, the system of balance of power, war, formal diplomatic relations and international organizations) which contribute to the effectiveness of these social rules.

The rules and the principles of international society are mixed with the rules and institutions of international politics. Indeed, when a social rule is violated, the instrument to compel the State that has committed the violation is, as a last resort, coercion by great powers. However, the dilemma between intervention and sovereignty to maintain the international political order has been the centre of the debate in international relations for years.

1.2 Intervention vs. sovereignty

The traditional Westphalian notion of sovereignty confers absolute author-ity to individual States to maintain domestic order within their borders and command the resources necessary to conduct effective relations with other States outside their own jurisdiction (Lyons and Mastanduno, 1995). This notion intended the concept of sovereignty to be an inviolable right of the State. This conception was overcome in 2001 with the formulation of the so-called Responsibility to Protect norm. However, to understand how far we have come, the best place to begin is with the United Nations (UN) Charter of 1945. After the Second World War, the UN founders were deeply concerned with the problem of States waging war against each other. This is the reason why the Charter produced a quite astonishing innovation as it outlawed the use of force, with the only exception being self-defence in confronting an attack, and with authorization from the UN Security Coun-cil (UNSC) (UNSC, 1945). This new international institution was given unprecedented authority to act in case of threats to international peace and security. On the matter, however, of the application of external force in response to an internal catastrophe, the Charter language made a clear state-ment of the principle of non-interference. 'Nothing contained in the present Charter shall authorize the UN to intervene in matters which are essentially within the domestic jurisdiction of any State' (UNSC, 1945 – Art 2/7). The Cold War and the large increase in UN membership during the decoloniza-tion era reinforced the inclination to read the Charter as very limited in its reach.

The fragile newborn States saw the non-intervention norm as one of their few defences against threats and pressures from more powerful interna-tional actors seeking to promote their own economic and political interests. This was extremely inhibiting to the development of any sense of obliga-tion to respond in an effective way to situations of catastrophic internal human rights violations (Evans, 2006). One big agreed-upon exception to the non-intervention principle was the Genocide Convention of 1948. How-ever, nothing much was done to give practical force and effect to the plain terms. Other relevant instruments were the Universal Declaration of Human Rights and the 1966 Conventions on Civil and Political Rights as well as Economic, Social, and Cultural Rights. In terms of implementation, the world remained at the rhetoric level, and the non-interference in domestic affairs principle kept on leading the behaviour of States. Despite the 1990s being characterized by intrastate conflicts, internal violence, civil wars, and gross violations of human rights perpetrated on a massive scale, the 'non-intervention trend' died very hard. Even when situations really needed some kind of response and the international community reacted through the UN, the response was often weak, slow, and incomplete. All this generated a very fierce debate about what came to be called 'humanitarian intervention'. On the one hand, there were those strongly claiming for the primacy of the concept of 'national sovereignty', and on the other hand, equally strong claims were made by those who fiercely argued for the right to intervene. The debate was fierce and unresolved throughout the 1990s (Evans, 2006).

1.3 Responsibility to protect

As noted previously, during the 1990s the international community witnessed an array of humanitarian crises. Although at that time international law already proscribed specific kinds of State behaviours within national borders, genocide, ethnic cleansing, mass atrocities, and mass internal displacement of citizens were still happening. As a result, in 1999 Kofi Annan challenged the international community to develop a way of reconciling the twin principles of sovereignty and the protection of fundamental human rights. In 2001 the International Commission on Intervention and State Sovereignty (ICISS) provided a report on the new concept of the so-called 'Responsibility to Protect' (R2P), which was based on the 'responsible sovereignty' principle (ICISS, 2001). This norm entailed a shift from the idea of 'sovereignty as control' to the concept of 'sovereignty as responsibility' (first presented by Francis Deng and Roberta Cohen in the early 1990s). The underlying reason for sovereignty became the protection of people's most fundamental rights from egregious violations. This notion overcame the Westphalian concept of sovereignty, based on the 'non-interference' principle, conceived primarily as the right to act within national borders without being internationally accountable.

According to the R2P norm, although national governments are responsible for their citizens, when a State is unwilling or unable to protect its own people from gross violations of human rights, the responsibility shifts to the international community (ICISS, 2001). R2P imposed a responsibility on States not to harm and also to pro-actively protect their populations, along with placing a responsibility on the wider international community to engage in an appropriately authorized and multilateral action (including, when needed, coercive force) to protect those populations if the particular States involved cannot or will not fulfil their responsibility. R2P was conceived on three key points: Responsibility to Prevent, Responsibility to React, and Responsibility to Rebuild (ICISS, 2001). The Responsibility to Prevent imposed on States and on the international community the obligation to prevent large-scale loss of lives through different avenues. Primary, the responsibility fell on the sovereign State, but even at this earlier stage the international community had important responsibilities. Responsibility to Prevent applied both to the root cause of conflicts and to their direct prevention. Root causes can include poverty, repression, and failures of distributive justice (ICISS, 2001). For this reason, the ICISS' report noted in particular the international community's responsibilities regarding development assistance and the removal of damaging restrictive trade policies. Responsibility to engage in diplomacy and mediation were also emphasized as the development of 'early warning procedures' (Breakey, 2011). The Responsibility to React was meant to trigger when prevention fails. It included non-interventionist measures (i.e. target sanctions). The ICISS put forward six criteria for legitimizing intervention even without the consent of the State in question, i.e. right authority, right intention, just cause, last resort, proportional means, and reasonable prospects of success. Intervention had to follow the authorization of the UNSC and it had to be triggered by a large-scale loss of life and/or 'ethnic cleansing', produced by a deliberate State action or a failed State situation. It had to require that all other paths for resolutions (such as diplomatic and non-military tools) had been explored. Moreover, the intention behind the intervention had to aim at reducing human suffering and military intervention should have not been greater than that required to accomplish that objective (ICISS, 2001). Finally, the Responsibility to Rebuild was thought to ensure that, post-intervention, the State was left in such a condition that it would not swiftly return to hostilities and renewed threats to civilians.

The Responsibility to Rebuild included 'Disarmament, Demobilization, and Reintegration' of local armed forces plus measures to prevent the so-called 'reverse ethnic-cleansing' and the safe and secure return of refugees (Breakey, 2011). Thanks to the determination of UN Secretary General Kofi Annan and other R2P advocates, Responsibility to Protect became one of the topics at the 2005 UN Millennium Summit and was included in the UN World Summit Outcome Document. This document introduced some changes. Firstly, it narrowed the focus on intervention (reducing it just to cases of genocide, war crimes, ethnic cleansing, and crimes against humanity), without mentioning explicitly the Responsibility to Rebuild present in the ICISS report. It did not adopt ICISS criteria for UNSC deliberations concerning the use of force. Moreover, it introduced a 'case-by-case' basis for deciding to intervene and it used the term 'preparedness' rather than 'responsibility' in reference to UNSC action (Breakey, 2011). In 2009, the UN Implementation Report on R2P clarified the concept of Responsibility to Protect and its various operational aspects. The goal was not to reinterpret or renegotiate the conclusions of the World Summit but to find ways of implementing its decisions in a fully faithful and consistent manner (UN Secretary General [UNSG], 2009). It introduced a 'three pillars' approach and military intervention lost much of its centrality. The first pillar dealt with the protection responsibilities of the State; the second referred to international capacity and State-building, while pillar three was about 'timely and decisive response'. The first two pillars delineated the preventive activities required by the State and the international community, whereas the third pillar put emphasis on pacific measures rather than military action. It described R2P as narrow in scope but deep in response, eliciting a wide variety of actions on the part of various agents in order to prevent the four crimes. In addition, it did not provide a sequence in moving from one pillar to another; R2P must be applied flexibly in the face of different circumstances. In 2015, the UN Secretary General's report 'A vital and enduring commitment: Implementing the R2P' reaffirmed the importance of the Responsibility to Protect norm, stating that at a national level, member States must make atrocity crime prevention and response a priority. They must undergo national risk assessment and articulate a comprehensive strategy for domestic and foreign policy in order to enhance national ability for atrocity prevention. It stressed the need to expand focal point networks, to connect responsive and flexible funding for preventative action to early warning mechanisms, and to conduct regular deliberations on best practices for atrocity crime prevention and response.

According to this report, member States must share regionally the lessons learned and ensure that atrocity crime prevention and response is consistently embedded in discussions at the regional institutions. At the international level, member States need to provide military and civilian capabilities to UN peace operations[2] that enable rapid and flexible response, ensure that post-conflict peace-building measures are tailored to atrocity crime risk, and work to expand efforts to prevent violent extremism and violence by non-State armed groups. It is important to note that R2P is not applicable to small-scale war crimes, institutionalized discrimination, disappearance, and sexual violence (all of which may occur during peacetime) but only to these crimes when they occur on a 'mass scale' (Breakey, 2011). More than his predecessors, the dominance of the sponsorship of Kofi Annan on the issues of human rights and humanitarian interventions is often regarded as the antecedent of the R2P principle. Its intellectual trajectory is, however, firmly rooted in the normative agenda of 'sovereignty as responsibility' put forward by Francis Deng and Roberta Cohen in the early 1990s (Weiss, 2006 cited in Okeke, 2008). The re-characterization of sovereignty as responsibility ostensibly prompted by the challenges to international peace and security in the post-Cold War era, suggested by Deng and his collaborators, sought to offer a normative benchmark for both national governments and the international community in their respective responsibilities (Deng, Rothchild, and Zartmann, 1996). Then, in 2001, the ICISS Report offered a similar conceptualization on State sovereignty. Despite all the evident limits of this norm, the critiques, and the fact that it is not innovative (as it draws heavily on previous scholarships), yet of significance and undoubtedly new is the attempt by the ICISS Report to elaborate the R2P norm upon the notion of a logical continuum of responsibility before, during, and after assaults on civilians (Weiss, 2006 cited in Okeke, 2008). This research focuses on the preventative part of the norm, specifically on the prevention of genocide among the four crimes addressed by R2P.

1.4 Prevention and early warning

The ICISS Report identified prevention as the single most important dimension of the R2P doctrine and, as noted before, stated that prevention option should always be exhausted before forceful military action is contemplated (ICISS, 2001). An emphasis on prevention is also evident in the UNSG's 2009 Report on the Implementation of R2P. It advocated the creation of a joint office for the UN Special Advisor on R2P and a UN Special Advisor on the Prevention of Genocide. Furthermore, the follow-up report in 2010 explicitly focussed on enhancing the UN's capacity for early warning and assessment (UNSG, 2010). It stressed that peaceful and preventive measures are effective if implemented early and if tailored to specific circumstances. It concluded by saying that early warning and assessment are critical in this pursuit (UNSG, 2010). It further stated that assisting those States that are under stress, before crises and conflict break out, will require early warning and impartial assessment mechanisms (UNSG, 2010). More recently, in a speech marking the first decade of the R2P, Ban Ki-moon declared 2012 as 'the year of prevention', designating it as one of the five generational themes for the UN (Ban Ki-moon, 2012).

In 2015, the Panel on United Nations Peace Operations stated that the UN has not invested enough on addressing root causes of conflict and that it must do this in partnership with others whilst strengthening its own capacities to undertake prevention work, including through inclusive and equitable development. In addition, it has admitted that resources for prevention have been scarce and the UN is often too slow to engage with emerging crises, while prevention of armed conflict is perhaps the greatest responsibility of the international community (HIPPO Report, 2015). Finally, the panel has declared that the UN must invest in its own capacities to undertake prevention and mediation and its capacity to assist others, particularly at the national and regional level, and that the UNSC, supported by the Secretariat, should seek to play an earlier role in addressing emerging conflicts and must do so with impartiality. It stated that at the global level, the UN must mobilize a new international commitment to prevent conflict and to mobilize partnership to support political solutions. It must find ways to draw on the knowledge and resources of others beyond the UN system through civil society, community, religious, youth and women groups, and the global business community.

Whereas a rich literature exists on how early warning and response should be carried out, very little is known about how early warning actually happens, especially in field-based systems. Consequently there is some scepticism about the entire concept of early warning among outsiders. The primary conceptual challenge revolves around the central issue that the added value of early warning is still unproven. That is due to two facts:

- that predictions have not been accurate in the past (or important events were not foreseen); and
- that operational responses have been inadequately linked to warnings.

Moreover, early warning methods have not demonstrated how they can engage with current high profile threats (e.g. organized crime, drugs, or terrorism) (Matveeva, 2006).

It is both politically and normatively desirable to act to prevent mass atrocity crimes from being committed rather than to react after they are already underway. Among other things, good prevention allows the international community, the involved actors to avoid the unending tension between the protection of individuals from the systematic violation of human rights and the protection of State sovereignty from external interference.

The R2P framework emphasizes that a focus on prevention will not only help to minimize human misery and human rights abuses, but can also yield tangible financial benefits (Bond and Sherret, 2006). Preventive strategies associated with R2P should aim at 'attacks directed at any population, committed in a widespread or systematic manner, in furtherance of a State or organizational policy, irrespective of the existence of discriminatory intent or an armed conflict' (Rome Statute, 1998 – Art. 8). Basically, prevention rests on three principles:

- early reaction to signs of disorder;
- a comprehensive, balanced approach to alleviate the pressures of risk factors to resolve the underlying root causes of violence; and
- extended efforts to resolve the underlying root causes of violence.

The common prevention agenda includes 'structural prevention' (security, governance, economic, social measures, and human rights) and 'direct prevention' (early warning, diplomatic measures, inducements, sanctions, and legal and military measures). Targeted strategies are designed to change either the incentives or situation of those contemplating or planning mass atrocity crimes, as well as the vulnerability of potential victims. Systemic strategies, by contrast, seek to mitigate risk factors and build resilience in a broader group of States that exhibit some of the so-called root causes of mass atrocity crimes (Welsh and Sharma, 2013). Atrocity prevention requires tailored engagement because the relationship between armed conflict and mass atrocities is highly complex and yet not well understood. In fact, the strong correlation between the two phenomena implies a direct link; however, not all conflicts give rise to mass atrocities and many atrocities occur in the absence of armed struggle.

In his report on 'R2P and Early Warning' (2010), UN Secretary General Ban Ki-moon noted that R2P crimes do not occur only within contexts of armed conflict and furthermore, these crimes have to be understood and recognized as possibly having different preconditions to generalized armed conflict. In fact, while a large majority of the episodes of mass killing observed since 1945 occurred within the context of armed conflict, at least a third of cases did not. There exists a significant number of cases where mass atrocities were committed in peacetime (or after an episode involving conflict). Only one out of ten of every reported civilian deaths tends to occur in the context of armed conflict with the majority taking place outside official combat zones (attributed, for example, to government repression or a State's failure to regulate violence). Besides, some instances of mass atrocities occur under the cover of armed conflict but are not directly linked either to the causes of that conflict or to the conduct of civil war (Geneva Declaration on Armed Violence and Development, 2011). Therefore, it is not to assume that efforts to prevent or resolve conflict will always simultaneously reduce the likelihood of mass atrocity crimes. Besides, whereas strategies to prevent or resolve conflicts generally aim at the elimination or avoidance of violence and the use of force, the prevention of mass atrocities may require military means. In addition, armed conflict is regulated but not proscribed by international law, whereas mass atrocities are outlawed as crimes (Welsh and Sharma, 2013). While armed conflict involves parties to a conflict, individuals in particular roles and positions commit mass atrocity crimes against other individuals. These acts represent a socially stigmatized behaviour that is condemned by the international community. For these and other reasons, the path towards developing effective atrocity prevention measures is likely to encounter a number of barriers along the way. Some of them might be the lack of political will to act before a crisis develops, and the resistance of many States towards preventive measures that would potentially infringe on their sovereignty.

Moreover, the added value of early warning is yet to be proven, operational responses are insufficiently linked to warning, attracting attention to low-profile conflicts remains a problem, and early warning methods have not shown how they can engage with current high profile threats (i.e. terrorism). In addition, not only is the transfer from macro-level political early warning to micro-level citizen-based warning and response system too slow, but early warning systems are expensive; early warning projects must demonstrate a clear return on investment to donors (Matveeva, 2006).

Atrocity prevention can also be challenged, according to the R2P report, by the inherently intrusive character of certain preventive strategies, the lack of funds available for preventive efforts, the dangers of exacerbating domestic tensions through increased international involvement, and the difficulty of mobilizing political will before a crisis becomes apparent (ICISS, 2001).

A key challenge facing any preventive agenda is creating a credible and authoritative mechanism for assessing the probability that crimes will be committed. Preventive measures (particularly those which are coercive) will be resisted when the approach to assessing risk factors is contested and when the body which assesses the potential for mass atrocity crimes is viewed as biased or lacking in relevant capacity or expertise. A second challenge is the belief of many scholars and practitioners that every mass atrocity situation is unique and requires tailor-made solutions. Nevertheless, while an appreciation of particular regional and local dynamics is critical, many of the most promising preventive tools such as finding or monitoring missions, satellite surveillance, mediation, targeted sanctions, or no-fly zones require already existing structures, skills, and technology if they are to be applied in a timely and effective fashion. Among the different tools of prevention, this research analyses early warning mechanisms of genocide prevention.

1.5 Early warning: describing the object under analysis

Early warning systems were first used for the purpose of predicting natural disasters and stock market crashes. In the 1980s, with the introduction of models to predict famine and potential refugee flow, early warning was first introduced into humanitarian affairs. It primarily aimed at alerting relief agencies of impeding humanitarian crises to allow for contingency planning and ensure the timely provision of adequate food, shelter, and medication (Piza-Lopez and Schmeild, 2002). In light of the immense human suffering as a result of violent conflicts and due to costly post-conflict emergency requirements, humanitarian early warning has lately developed knowledge-based models to help decision makers formulating coherent political strategies to prevent or limit the destructive effects of violent conflicts (Piza-Lopez and Schmeild, 2002). The emphasis is on 'anticipating' the potential for crises rather than on 'forecasting' it. According to extensive literature on the topic (Gurr, 1996; Rusu, 1997; Adelman, 1998; Schmeidl and Jenkins, 1998; Forum for Early Warning and Early Response [FEWER], 1999; Interdisciplinary Program of Research on Root Causes of Human Rights Violations [PIOOM], 1999), despite the different given definitions on early warning, a number of common elements may be underscored. These are the collection of information using specific indicators, the analysis of information (i.e. attaching meaning to indicators, setting it into context, and recognizing crisis development), the formulation of the 'best and worst' case scenarios and response options, and finally communication to decision makers.

Today, early warning systems are playing a crucial role in the international arena, in identifying areas at risk of violent conflict and mass atrocities. The development of a multi-method approach has brought early warning analysis closer to anticipating rather than predicting crises that could lead to large-scale humanitarian disasters. Such analyses now increasingly focus on the grassroots level, working with major stakeholders and cooperating with local partners. What separates early warning from peace building and conflict mitigation is its implied proactive and not reactive character, with a focus on early rather than late action (Piza-Lopez and Schmeild, 2002). The element that makes early warning so important is that even if it does not always produce early reaction, early reaction is highly unlikely without early warning. Early action must be well-informed action; it needs sophisticated early warning and assessment capabilities. However, despite all the advancement reached in the field of early warning and risk assessment, according to the Early Warning Assessment and R2P Report (2010), some gaps in early warning and assessment still exist. There is an insufficient sharing of information and analysis among the actors and throughout the UN, and the existing mechanisms for gathering and assessing information for early warning do not analyse that information through an R2P lens, but rather view conflicts in broader terms. To these gaps, many scholars (Piza-Lopez and Schmeild, 2002; Bond and Sherret, 2012; Davis, Nkokora, and Teitt, 2015) added the 'gender-blind' nature of early warning assessment. Indeed, until recently, a gender perspective was completely absent from conflict and atrocity early warning systems and preventive response systems. This research places itself in this line of inquiry, suggesting that the analysis of genocide early warning practices would be improved if gender-based indicators were included. The reason behind this suggestion is the conviction that a gender-sensitive focus may enrich the understanding of factors that lead to genocide and thus improve early analysis and the formulation of response options.

1.6 Gender and early warning

Before going deeper in the topic, we need to define and clarify the key terms. The term 'gender', largely used since the 1970s, focuses on the socially constructed as opposed to biologically determined sex identities of men and women in societies. By definition, the term gender refers to both men and women. According to Woroniuk (1999), the goal of engendering society or politics is not a reversal of discrimination or an attempt to make men and women similar, but a means to attain equity through equal opportunities and life chances. As a consequence, 'engendering early warning' is not only concerned with including women into early warning systems, but on sensitizing the entire process by training both men and women on how to use gender analysis to fine-tune early warning and allow for a more appropriate and diverse range of response options. A 'gender-sensitive indicator' can be defined as an indicator that captures gender-related changes in society over time (Johnson, 1985 cited in Beck, 1999). While statistics disaggregated by sex provide 'factual information about the status of women, a gender-sensitive indicator provides direct evidence of the status of women, relative to some agreed normative standard of explicit reference group (i.e. men)' (Beck, 1999 p. 9).[3]

1.6.1 Gender in R2P and international documents

In the field of peace and security, there has been generally a tendency to view gender issues as irrelevant to the subject matter or at best a too costly and time-consuming 'extra-option' to deal with in times of crises. In matters of security and humanitarian interventions, for a long time common sense has not taken women's perspectives and needs into consideration. This appears also to be the case with the core R2P documents. Indeed, in 2001 the commissioners, consultations, and materials used to prepare the R2P report showed a distinct lack of gender awareness and the ICISS itself did not provide for equal participation of women. Given these factors, it is not surprising that the report is itself almost entirely gender-blind. The 108-page report mentions women only three times, and none of these references are in relation to the importance of including women in the process of recognizing their unique needs and contributions in conflict and post-conflict environments (Bond and Sherret, 2012). During this time, R2P has failed to incorporate gender perspectives and in particular the requirements of prevention, protection, and participation, as established in Resolution 1325 (2000) (Stamnes, 2012). In 2010, Resolution 1960 called to include specific gender indicators that could facilitate early warning for the prevention of mass atrocities, calling upon member States to improve their data collection and analysis in these areas. The UNSC approved the creation of the Inter-Agency Standing Committee on Women, Peace and Security, tasked with creating a strategic framework that would guide the development of MARA (Monitoring Analysis and Reporting Arrangements on Conflict-related Sexual Violence).

This led to the establishment of a UN Matrix of Early Warning Indicators of Conflict Related Sexual Violence to guide the actions of the UN Security Council to prevent, halt, and prosecute such crimes (Davis, Nkokora and Teitt, 2015). However, the fulfilment of this framework requires member States to provide data in relation to gender-specific indicators including specific acts of violence against women, implementation of international human rights law pertaining to gender equality, economic and social indicators for women, and UN-specific indicators for women in peacekeeping missions (UNSG, 2010). The UN set the target of ensuring that its early warning systems tasked with responding to escalating events (i.e. the UN High Commissioner for Refugees, the UN Department of Political Affairs, and UN Office for Humanitarian Affairs) include gender-specific indicators by 2014. It has also set gender-specific indicators to be included as standard across all the systems' early warning analysis by 2020 (UNSG, 2011). However, it seems that so far no discussion or even recognition of the shared interests in prevention and early warning between the Inter-Agency Standing Committee and the Office for the Prevention of Genocide and the R2P has been conducted. Moreover, all early warning frameworks focussed in MARA are on escalating acts of sexual violence and the perpetrators rather than the structural conditions that give rise to such acts (i.e. an early warning framework, which focusses on intervening variables that prevent as well as predict) (Davis, Nkokora and Teitt, 2015). The UN Secretary General, in his reports on R2P, has made two major references (in 2009 and 2013) to the need to direct more attention and research to record best practices in the alleviation of gender inequality and the promotion of gender empowerment to prevent mass atrocities, including SGBV (Sexual Gender-Based Violence, i.e. violence targeting individuals or groups on the basis of their gender) crimes. However, beyond these suggestions, there has been little direction on how to start building such knowledge. Moreover, the Office of the UN Secretary General's Special Adviser on the Prevention of Genocide and the Special Adviser for R2P have not addressed yet, the role of gender inequality and gendered violence in early warning frameworks (Davis, Nkokora and Teitt, 2015). On the basis of the preceding outline, the conclusion may be that gender has not been given the expected attention in either the formulation of the R2P norm or in early warning mechanisms. There has been a failure to connect the R2P and the WPS (Women, Peace, and Security) agenda (Bond and Sherret, 2012). One potential reason for the 'gender silence' in early warning analysis for mass atrocities may be that the primary focus has been on defining what modelling provides best predictive capacity, and what is to be 'tested' in these frameworks (i.e. ethnic minorities versus political-socio-economic targeting) (Ulfelder, 2011).

After all, the concept of an early warning framework is still relatively new. Another potential explanation for the silence could be that the need for gender-focussed early warning has received only sporadic interest from the UNSC and that interest has been limited to its thematic agenda on WPS into other Security Council themes, missions, and agendas (Aroussi, 2011). This is particularly highlighted in discussions about sexual violence in the UNSC where there has been active political opposition to discussions about widespread and systematic sexual violence in conflicts that are not already on the agenda of the Security Council, despite precedents in other thematic areas, specifically in discussion of children in armed conflict (UNSC, 2012). The argument for including women's perspectives in R2P preventive practices does not hinge upon the fact that they are more affected by mass atrocities than men are.[4] Their experiences should be considered because they represent half of the world's population and thus half of what needs to be understood. The need to broaden the lens to observe reality in a way that also captures women's experiences is the reason why there is the need to engender early warning mechanisms. No solution can be found without dealing with the whole picture; the current early warning mechanisms and the R2P preventive pillar might become more effective by integrating gender indicators into their frameworks. In dealing with mass atrocity prevention, it should be considered that women, their experiences, and their roles are part of what we are looking for. Engendering early warning mechanisms aims at making them 'earlier' and more comprehensive, and preventive actions more permanent and effective.

1.6.2 Gender-sensitive early warning

According to the existing literature, gender-sensitive early warning systems should include changes in gender equality, violation of women's human rights, domestic violence, trafficking of women, sex-specific migration patterns, women's access to education, women's access to reproductive healthcare, and fertility rates, because there is a correlation between these factors and violence. Indeed, research suggests that States with a lower percentage of women in parliament are more likely to use military violence to settle disputes (Caprioli, 2000). A five-percent decrease in the proportion of women in parliament renders a State nearly five (4.91) times as likely to resolve international disputes using military violence. Also, female suffrage and the percentage of women in the labour force show statistical significance in explaining State bellicosity. The correlation between gender inequality and levels of violence, wars, and violation of human rights and the reasons for this correlation will be deeper analysed in Chapter 2. However, this correlation leads us to consider the influence that these elements may have on the eruption of violence within a country. In 2002, Piza-Lopez and Schmeidl showed how gender-based indicators can be used in conjunction with wider socio-political analyses.

In analysing early warning mechanisms for preventing armed conflict, they started from three general elements, i.e. the root or structural/systemic causes, the proximate causes, and the intervening factors. Their work showed how possible and useful it might be to engender the indicators of early warning mechanisms to better understand the causes that generally lead to the eruption of an armed conflict. For the purpose of engendering the indicators of the root causes (i.e. general and deep-rooted background conditions), their hypothesis is that the more inclusive a society is, the less likely it will resort to force as a means of conflict resolution. Research suggests that cultures which limit women's access to resources (political, economic, and social) and decision-making power, and which characterize men as superior to women, treat women as property, and accept domestic violence as a norm, are more prone to repression and violent conflict in the public arena. This is the reason why, according to these scholars, indicators of structural inequality between men and women should be considered in early warning. Together with root causes, proximate causes (i.e. medium term conditions and emerging socio-political and economic trends) can create sufficient conditions for armed conflict. About proximate causes, Piza-Lopez and Schmeild (2002) suggested that gender analysis might draw attention to deviating behavioural patterns and demographic trends, highlighting dysfunctionalities that could be precursors to armed conflict. In this case, the reduction in the status of women, discrimination against women (but also men who refuse to go to battle), media scapegoating, violations of women's human rights, and virulent attacks on women may be direct precursors of further repression and violent conflict because unequal social hierarchies, including gender hierarchies, inequality, and oppression, are often characteristics of societies that are prone to or embroiled in conflict (Tickner, 1999). Thus, they concluded that when a shift in gender roles occurs in society from more open to more closed, this could also be a warning signal of an overall move towards repression and conflictual behaviour. Finally, in analysing the intervening factors or 'accelerators' (i.e. those factors that can either increase or decrease the likelihood of an armed conflict) (Harff, 1998; Ahmed and Kassinis, 1998), they suggested it is crucial to consider organizations working to diminish violence, which includes the grassroots level where women and women's organizations are active.

Thus, other signals of a pattern moving toward violent conflict might be considered, such as:

- the resistance to women's participation in peace processes and peace negotiations on the part of guerrilla/armed groups, warlords, and governments;
- the lack of presence of women in civil society organizations; and
- the lack of women's organizations in addition to the 'usual' elements (i.e. media scapegoating of women, engagement of women in shadow war economies as prostitutes, and the growth of discriminatory movements such as fundamentalism).

On the other hand, regarding engendering early warning indicators for mass atrocity prevention, recent research (Davis, Nkokora, and Teitt, 2015) showed that gender-specific indicators might be useful as traditional non-gender measures for early warning of imminent mass atrocities. That research looked at the countries deemed at risk of mass atrocities (R2P crimes) by genocide prevention and Genocide Watch lists, and then compared it with a set of gender-specific root causes indicators, which generated a gendered 'preconditions' list based on the indicators identified by Piza-Lopez and Schmeild (2002). The results showed that inequality indices alone were likely to identify risk of sexual gender-based violence atrocities. This led the scholars to conclude that related early warning frameworks must regularly engage with gender-specific indicators.

1.7   Adding gender-sensitive indicators in early warning frameworks for genocide prevention

In Chapter 2, an excursus of different models of genocide prevention and early warning will be presented in detail; however, analysing the different early warning and prevention models regarding genocide, the conclusion is that there is a lack of gender-sensitive indicators. Despite the fact that legal developments in relation to genocide refer to gender-specific crimes (i.e. mass rape, forced sterilization and abortions, forced impregnation, and forced marriage), neither two of the most highly sourced and respected annual risk analyses (i.e. those produced by Barbara Harff and Gregory Stanton) analyse gender-specific indicators (Butcher et al., 2012). Nor it has been taken into consideration whether a focus on such indicators or prior existence of widespread and systemic SGVB and gender inequality in a country may affect the country risk lists produced. In addition, it should be considered an element of 'concern' that women-focussed political, economic, and social indicators remain relatively untested as factors that may prevent mass atrocities (Davis, Nkokora, and Teitt, 2015). Given these reasons and the positive results showed in the literature presented earlier, this research aims at upgrading the work on genocide prevention, suggesting the addition of gender-sensitive indicators to early warning mechanisms. UN Women raised arguments for early warning frameworks to include gender-specific indicators in 2014 (UN Women, 2014). A series of UNIFEM-led studies used the Piza-Lopez and Schmeild (2002) model to explore the utility of local information gathering for early warning about escalating violence (i.e. identifying SGVB early to prevent it from becoming widespread and systematic) (Moser, 2007). If one of the best predictors of a country's peacefulness is its level of violence against women, there should be efforts to analyse how women's status in society relates to violence and, more generally, to the risk of genocide (Hudson et al., 2012). In particular, the inclusion of information about women's human rights and violence against women into existing early warning frameworks on genocide prevention should improve the capacity to predict not only widespread and systematic SGBV but also other atrocity crimes (Palermo and Peterman, 2011; von Joeden-Forgey, 2012). The process of engendering early warning by integrating a gender perspective into all stages of early warning of genocide prevention at all levels, not confining gender issues to a single process, can improve existing approaches of information collection, analysis, and response formulation. The integration of gender into current early warning practices would lead to more practical, accurate, and realistic approaches. In addition, while becoming more comprehensive, they could also become more effective by ensuring that the concerns of men and women are equally considered, to benefit men as well as women (Piza-Lopez and Schmeild, 2002). It might also provide a better understanding of unequal social hierarchies, including gender hierarchies, inequality, and oppression, which are often characteristics of societies that are prone to or embroiled in genocidal violence. It would make gender equality and equity an essential consideration in the building of sustainable peace and the reconstruction of democratic processes. Engendering early warning might push analysts to ask new questions relating to the conditions of life among different classes, age groups, identity groups, etc. at different levels of society. The consequence is that the inclusion and mainstreaming of these considerations into the agendas of relevant policy makers at an earlier stage might lead to a more integrated and comprehensive understanding of the realities on the ground.

In turn, this might lead to 'earlier' early warning and/or longer-term perspectives that introduce conflict prevention into development planning (Leonhardt, 2000). Experts believe that the 'advisory' component of early warning which tells policy makers how events may unfold and what actions could be taken decreases the warning-response gap and political will problem, particularly if lack of political will is linked with not knowing what to do rather than not wanting to do anything (Piza-Lopez and Schmeild, 2002). However, simply to work with gender-sensitive indicators is not enough to engender true early warning. The ultimate challenge is to link micro-level responses to the macro-picture of genocide (Piza-Lopez and Schmeild, 2002). Indeed, engendering early warning illuminating micro-level processes is not only beneficial for anticipating genocide early in the process of violence escalation, but it might also lead to more 'fine-tuned' policy recommendations (i.e. reducing gender inequality and SGVB as a means to reduce the risk of genocide). In addition, without gender-analysis, old pre-genocide norms may be inadvertently perpetuated and render women even more vulnerable than before the genocide.

Notes

1 *Paradigms* are one or more general conceptions of reality (Kuhn, 1962).
2 The term 'UN Peace Operations' embraces a broad suite of tools managed by the UN Secretariat. These instruments range from special envoys and mediators, political missions (including peace-building missions), regional preventive diplomacy offices, observation missions (both ceasefire and electoral missions), small, technical specialist missions (such as electoral support missions), multidisciplinary operations both large and small drawing on civilian, military and police personnel to support peace process implementation (even including transitional authorities with governance functions), as well as advance missions for planning. All these missions draw upon expertise mobilized by the Secretariat, including mediation and electoral specialists and human rights, rule of law, gender, police and military experts (Report of the High Level Independent Panel on UN Peace Operations [HIPPO Report], 2015).
3 For example, to say that 60% of women in a given country are literate is a gender statistic, but to say that 60% of women in a given country are literate compared to 82% of men is a gender-sensitive indicator (Piza-Lopez and Schmeild, 2002).
4 Although entire communities suffer the consequence of armed conflict, women and girls are particularly affected because of their status in society and their sex (UN Women, 2000).

2 Genocide and gender equality

2.1 Gender inequality and violence

Many scholars have argued that a domestic environment of gender inequality and violence results in greater likelihood of violence both at national and international levels. According to the existing literature (Caprioli, 2000, 2003, 2005; Boyer and Caprioli 2001a,b; Caprioli and Trumbore 2003, 2005, 2006; Fish, 2002; Piza-Lopez and Schmeild, 2002; Francis, 2004; Melander, 2005a; Sobek, Abouharb, and Ingram, 2006), there is a correlation between levels of violence, international violence, intrastate armed conflicts, civil wars, and gender inequality. Critiques to this line of inquiry were moved during time, and they regarded the fact that this literature generally suggests correlation rather than causation. The links between gender-based violence and conflict are complex to separate out from other factors, as GBV causes and consequences are influenced by many factors and rooted in context. Moreover, the nature of the relationship between the levels of structural (institutional) GBV and conflict is not clear, even if studies quantitatively prove a strong correlation (Herbert, 2014). Data difficulties are also highlighted as a key limitation. In addition, GBV is present also in those countries with high levels of gender equality (Herbert, 2014). Finally, GBV is considered a form of violent conflict in itself, so rather than being seen as an indicator of future conflict, it should be seen as indicator that conflict is already happening (Saferworld, 2014). However, despite the critiques, the results are substantial. States with high fertility rates (i.e. the number of births per woman) are more likely to use force in international disputes. A decrease in fertility rate by one third makes a State nearly five (4.67) times less likely to use a military solution to settle international disputes (Caprioli, 2000).[1] Civil wars are much more likely in States with high fertility rates (94.3% of States experiencing coded civil war have a fertility rate of 3.01 or higher) (Caprioli, 2003). A simple statistically significant cross tabulation shows that 87.9% of PRIO/

UPPSALA coded internal conflict is within States having a fertility rate of 3.01 or more (Caprioli, 2003). States with high fertility rates are nearly twice (1.083) as likely to experience internal conflict than those with low fertility rates, while controlling for other possible causes of internal conflict (Caprioli, 2005). Fertility rate is a statistically significant indicator because it encompasses a broad range of concepts including level of education, available economic opportunities, political rights, and overall social status. It best measures a woman's overall status by capturing not only an aspect of education, but also a measure of self-empowerment through control over her own life.

Regarding the rate of female representation in parliament, research shows that a higher rate of female participation corresponds to a lower State level of human rights abuse. The percentage of women in parliament has a benign effect on State human rights behaviour directly as well as in interaction with the level of institutional democracy (Melander, 2005b). States having a lower percentage of women in parliament are also more likely to use military violence to settle disputes. A 5% decrease in the proportion of women in parliament renders a State nearly five (4.91) times more likely to resolve international disputes using military violence (Caprioli, 2005). Finally, gender equality measured as the percentage of women in parliament and the ratio of female-to-male higher education attainment is associated with lower levels of armed conflict within a country (Melander, 2005a). It may actually have a pacifying effect on State behaviour, reducing the likelihood of interstate war (Caprioli, 2000).

Another significant indicator is the participation of women in the labour force. It can be interpreted as the extent to which women are integrated into the public sphere and other forms of participation such as voting or political activism (Piza-Lopez and Schmeild, 2002). Research shows that increasing the proportion of women in the labour force by 5% renders a State nearly five (4.95) times less likely to use military force to resolve international conflict (Caprioli, 2002). Moreover, States with 10% women in the labour force are nearly thirty (29.1) times more likely to experience internal conflict than States with 40% women in the labour force, while controlling for other possible causes of internal conflict (Caprioli, 2005). Female suffrage is also a significant predictor of State bellicosity. Given two States, the State having twice the number of years of female suffrage will be nearly five (4.49) times more likely to resolve international disputes without military violence (Caprioli, 2000). Finally, societies with high levels of family violence are more likely to be involved in wars and to rely on violent conflict resolution compared to societies with lower levels of family violence (Levinson 1989, Brumfield 1994, Erchak and Rosenfeld 1994, cited in Caprioli, 2000).

In general, we can conclude that there is a correlation between gender equality and the presence or absence of armed conflict (both intrastate and interstate), human rights abuses, the likelihood of becoming involved in militarized intrastate disputes and the likelihood of using violence first during militarized interstate disputes. An increase in gender equality leads to a decrease in conflict levels and human rights abuse. Other research (Ballif-Spanvill et al., 2008) quantitatively analysed the 'physical security of women' across countries. The authors compiled their own Physical Security of Women Index (PSOW) by examining the prevalence of domestic violence, rape, marital rape, and murder of women in the studied nations, plus another variant index that includes the degree to which the preference for sons is present within society. The results of that research showed a strong and statistically significant relationship between the physical security of women and the relative peacefulness of States. It showed that countries that practice high levels of violence against women and girls (i.e. household violence, female infanticide, and sex-selective abortion) are more likely to experience armed conflict than those that do not. The same authors in 2012 measured gender equality in 175 States and concluded that although it is not possible to establish a causal relationship, data proved that:

- the higher the level of violence against women, the more likely a State is to be non-compliant with international norms;
- the higher the level of violence against women, the worse a State's relations with neighbouring countries;
- the larger the gender gap, the more likely the State is to be involved in inter- and intrastate conflict, and to use violence first in a conflict; and
- the higher the level of violence against women, the less peacefully the State will behave in the international system.

They also noted adverse effects on State security from abnormal sex ratios (favouring males), polygamy, and inequitable family law, among other gendered aggressions. This is consistent with the findings of Sobek Abouharb and Ingram (2006) that domestic norms centred on equality and respect for human rights reduce international conflicts. Another part of the literature showed a correlation between high levels of interpersonal violence and the so-called honour cultures (focusing on controlling women, their bodies, and sexuality and restricting their freedom of movement) (Baller, Zevenberg and Messner, 2009; Brown, Osterman and Barnes, 2009; Somech and Elizur, 2009; Korteweg and Yurdakul, 2010; Ijzerman and Cohen, 2011; Inglis and MacKeogh, 2012). According to Cockburn (2010), patriarchal gender relations are also partly responsible for causing and perpetuating conflict at all levels of society. In particular, patriarchal gender relations intersect with economic and ethno-national power relations in perpetuating a tendency towards armed conflict in societies. Gender inequality is also correlated with a number of State-level indicators including indices of corruption, child survival/mortality and malnutrition, GDP per capita, 'global competitiveness ranking', and economic growth rates (Esteve-Volart, 2000; King and Mason, 2001). There is also a hypothesis that oppression of females provides the template for other types of oppression, including authoritarism (Ekvall, 2000; Caprioli, 2003; Caprioli, 2005). According to the presented literature, societies that are more equitable are supposed to be more peaceful because women have a say over matters of war and peace and they are generally more averse to war than men are. Alternatively, societies that are more equitable may be more peaceful because the norms of inviolability and respect that define equal relations between women and men are carried over to wider societal relations. The first explanation is based on the assumption that female aversion to violence is inherent in the essential nature of women (*essentialist argument*), while the second one emphasizes that gender roles and their accompanying attitudes are socially constructed (*constructivist argument*).

The essentialist argument argues that the aversion to violence and preference for peaceful methods of dealing with conflicts come together with the unique female ability to give birth and the skills of mothering transmitted from experienced mothers to girls and women. In line with this reasoning, numerous studies show that women tend to express attitudes that are more negative to the use of force in various contexts (Frankovic 1982; Smith 1984; Togeby 1994; Tessler and Warriner 1997 cited in Melander, 2005a). According to the constructivist argument, however, female aversion and male predisposition to violence have less to do with the biological sexes and more to do with certain socially constructed definitions of femininity and masculinity with which people identify (Tickner 1992, 2001; Goldstein, 2001; Fish, 2002 cited in Melander, 2005a). Two central themes in the construction of gender roles reoccur throughout more or less all known cultures:

- boys and men are prepared for their potential function as warriors while women are assigned the roles of caring and nursing; and
- gender roles legitimize the subordination of women.

Indeed, traditional gender identities can be drivers of conflict as men are framed as protectors and fighters, whereas women are seen as vulnerable and in need of protection (El-Bushra and Sahl, 2005). During periods of conflict, these identities can be accentuated and politicized (Goldstein, 2001). For instance, violent cattle raids in South Sudan are a tradition and rite of passage for men. However, when cattle are exchanged for girls and women, the raids also perpetuate conflict between communities and exacerbate violent abductions and revenge attacks (Safeworld and Conciliation Resources, 2014). Violent hypermasculinity can be indicative of tensions leading to conflict (Anderlini, 2006). However, it is not merely inequality or diversity that spurs intrastate violence but rather systemic discrimination. Socialization, gender stereotyping, and a constant threat of violence (all of which insidiously identify women as inferior) maintain structural violence (Bunch and Carrillo, 1998). Although women have become active agents with notable success in the struggle for equality, violence remains a component of relations between men and women and an enduring aspect of cultural violence that underscores gendered structural violence (Sideris, 2001). Gender is an integral aspect of structural violence, because gender forms the basis of structural inequality in all States. Although the power and the role of women vary across States, women have yet to gain full equality everywhere. Gender is a multifactored aspect of discrimination with issues of gender determining roles, power relationships, responsibilities, expectations, and access to resources (United Nations Population Fund [UNPFA], 2005). The intrusion of gender inequality throughout all aspects of human interaction thus creates the foundation for structural inequality. When an environment of structural violence supports and legitimizes societal tolerance of violence, the incidence of both inter- and intrastate violence may increase as violence becomes a way of life and a valid tool for setting disputes (Caprioli, 2005). Norms of violence and oppression that maintain gendered structural hierarchies may result in higher levels of intrastate violence by inuring people and providing the framework for justifying violence. States characterized by gender discrimination and structural hierarchy are permeated with norms of violence that make conflict more likely, because States usually replicate national politics patterns at the international level and apply the same norms in both contexts (Bonta, 1996; Maoz, 2003; Caprioli and Trumbore, 2006).

2.2 Gendered structural violence as one of the causes of genocide

This research aims at proving the main hypothesis regarding the possible correlation between gender equality and genocide, founded on Johan Galtung's theory of structural violence. As presented in the previous paragraph, a large part of literature shows that gender inequality increases the likelihood that a State will experience conflict. However, the possible correlation between gender equality and genocide remains untested. The key premise of my research is the statement made by Adam Jones in 2006, who argued that genocidal studies should 'move to incorporate an understanding of structural and institutional violence as genocidal mechanisms [. . .] discourse on genocide and structural/institutional violence deserves to move closer to the mainstream of genocide studies' (Jones, 2006 p. 47). Before going deeper into the topic, it is necessary to present what the theory of structural violence is about. According to Galtung (1975), structural violence is understood as systematic exploitation that becomes part of the social order. Basically, it exists when some groups, classes, genders, nationalities, etc. are assumed to have, and in fact do have, more access to goods, resources, and opportunities than other groups, classes, genders, nationalities, and so on, and this unequal advantage is built into the very social, political, and economic systems that govern societies, States, and the world. Structural violence causes direct violence (i.e. physical and/or verbal) and consequently, direct violence reinforces structural violence. Direct violence can take many forms. Galtung describes it as the 'avoidable impairment of fundamental human needs or life which makes it impossible or difficult for people to meet their needs or achieve their full potential' (1993 p. 106). Although Galtung focussed on structural violence in terms of economic inequality, his theory can be applied to other forms of structural violence. Structural violence has four basic components:

- exploitation, which is focussed on the division of labour with the benefits being asymmetrically distributed;
- penetration, which necessitates the control by the exploiters over the consciousness of the exploited, thus resulting in the acquiescence of the oppressed;
- fragmentation, which means that the exploited are separated from each other; and
- marginalization, in which the exploiters are a privileged class and have their own rules and form of interaction.

In applying Galtung's model of structural violence to women, Mary Caprioli (2003) found all four components of structural violence. In terms of exploitation, gender roles and expectations lead to different possibilities for personal development. The second element, penetration, is closely related to exploitation 'by providing a structure that produces extreme differentials in development of consciousness' (Caprioli, 2005 p. 164). Structural violence is maintained through socialization, gender stereotyping, and a constant threat of violence (Bunch and Carrillo, 1998), all of which identify women as inferior. Third, fragmentation results from women having fewer job opportunities outside the home that would allow participation and create a sense of efficacy (Pateman, 1970). Fragmentation also results from women having greater family responsibilities, thus minimizing leisure time that could otherwise be used to socialize, meet with other women, or become politically active. Finally, 'marginalization is the clear separation line between the two [in this case men and women], leaving no doubt as to who are first class and who are second-class' (Galtung, 1975 p. 265). Indeed, gendered hierarchies are indicative of a set of social practices, beliefs, ideas, values, and speech that promote male domination and superiority and female subordination and 'secondariness' (Rowbotham, 1983; Sideris, 2001). Thus, the intrusion of gender inequality throughout all aspects of human interaction creates the foundation for structural inequality. Structural inequality is in fact based on the subjugation and inequality (Dietz, 1985) that is rooted in hierarchy, domination, and the use of force (Brock-Utne, 1990). Finally, structural inequality generates structural violence, which is the cause of the eruption of direct violence. Gendered structural hierarchies, maintained by norms of violence and oppression, do not result just in a higher level of conflict (as presented in the previous chapter), but also have a role in explaining ethnic insurgencies (Caprioli, 2005). Thus, considering genocide to be a subset of intrastate conflict (and because, as presented previously, norms of intolerance and inequality have an incendiary impact on domestic behaviour by legitimizing violence as a tool of conflict resolution), by measuring gender equality within a country we might better foresee the eruption of genocidal violence.

2.3 Debating about genocide

Despite that genocide is not a twentieth century product, its definition is. Massacres and mass atrocities are not a 'modern' practice. They were the order of the day in antiquity, and colonization and imperialism provide many more- or less-successful examples of it. Humanity has always nurtured conceptions of social difference that generate a sense of 'in-group' versus 'out-group', as well as hierarchies of good and evil, superior and inferior, desirable and undesirable (Jones, 2006). However, conceptual accuracy is crucial when identifying a situation as being or not being genocide. As a concept, genocide was born in the turmoil of a world war in one of humanity's most dreadful centuries. Despite several decades of discussion and application, genocide is a term that is still misunderstood and often misapplied. Ever since it was first coined, there have been disputes about how it should be defined and interpreted. There is all manner of problems attached to defining genocide and the term is often misused when people describe human evil resulting in the death of a huge number of human beings. Sometimes genocide is used as synonymous with war. In popular consciousness, the first thing that can come to mind when thinking about genocide is killing on a vast scale.

Genocide is usually seen as related to brutal death, massive in type, and uncompromising in its choice of victims (Bartrop, 2014). However, as presented in Chapter 1, the relationship between armed conflict and genocide is highly complex and not well understood. The strong correlation between the two phenomena implies a direct link; however, not all conflicts give rise to genocide and many atrocities occur in the absence of armed struggle. There exist cases where genocide is committed in peacetime (or after an episode involving conflict). Genocide may occur under the cover of armed conflict but it may not be directly linked to either the causes of that conflict or to the conduct of civil war (see Chapter 1). There is no doubt that war contains within it the potential for a genocidal regime to realize its aims, and probably more easily than in peacetime. Yet war does not equate with genocide and the two terms should not be employed interchangeably (Bartrop, 2014). Genocide, in fact, is not merely a product of conflict. It usually stems from a long-standing obsession on the part of the perpetrators with the physical, political, social, psychological, religious, or cultural differences of the victim group. These differences are so great and irreconcilable that the perpetrator sees no solution to the situation except the elimination of the 'other' through mass annihilation. Another 'stereotype' of genocide is its link to religion (Bergen, 2006). To many people, the link between religion and genocide seems obvious, even though especially in the West organized religion has lost most or even all of its public power due to secularization. This link is actually not so obvious and scholars have attempted to identify and analyse such assumptions with historical specificity. Religion indeed is present in the UN Convention's definition of genocide only as one of the possible identifiers of the targets of attack. That religion might have something to do with the perpetrators of genocide is hinted at in the UN definition's focus on intention (UN General Assembly [UNGA], 1948), but it is not made explicit. Thus, one must be careful not to take this kind of correlation for granted. It is also important to outline the difference between genocide and ethnic cleansing, terms that too often are used interchangeably. As opposed to genocide, ethnic cleansing is intimately related with war, and all the recent instances of ethnic cleansing happened in the shadow of war (Das, 2006). War usually provides a cover for atrocities because war habituates people to brutality, and mechanisms of censorship silence any dissenting voices. The ideology of ethnic cleansing espouses a totalistic vision, i.e. very few exceptions are tolerated since the goal is to kill every person in the 'defined minority' (Das, 2006). According to Naimark (2001), genocide is the intentional killing of a part or all of an ethnic, religious, or national group; the murder of a people or peoples is the objective. The intention of ethnic cleansing is to remove a people and often all traces of it from a concrete territory. It is important to stress that genocide does not emerge out of nowhere. In all cases, there are always a number of preventable preliminary steps on the road to the ultimate 'solution' of a regime's alienation, isolation, and oppression prior to the decisive stage of a target group's destruction (Bartrop, 2014).

2.3.1 Defining the crime of genocide

To use the words of British Prime Minister Winston Churchill, until the Second World War, genocide was a 'crime without a name' (Jones, 2006 p. 8). In 1944, Polish-Jewish jurist, Raphael Lemkin, named the crime and placed it in a global-historical context, demanding also intervention and remedial action. He supported the coining of this new term with wide documentation. He settled on a neologism with both Greek and Latin roots: the Greek *genos* meaning race or tribe, and the Latin *cide* or killing. Thus, according to Lemkin, genocide was the intentional destruction of national groups based on their collective identity. By genocide, Lemkin meant the destruction of a nation or an ethnic group. It did not necessarily refer to the immediate destruction of a nation, except when accomplished by mass killing of all members of a nation. For Lemkin, genocide meant rather to signify a coordinated plan of different actions aimed at the destruction of essential foundations of the life of national groups with the aim of annihilating the groups themselves. The objectives of such a plan would be disintegration of the political and social institutions of culture, language, national feelings, religion, the economic existence of national groups, and the destruction of the personal security, liberty, health, dignity, and even the lives of the individuals belonging to such groups (Jones, 2006). He described two phases of genocide:

1   the destruction of the national pattern of the oppressed group; and
2   the imposition of the national pattern of the oppressor. The oppressor may make this imposition upon the oppressed population that is allowed to remain, or upon the territory alone after removal of the population and the colonization of the area.

His book *Axis Occupied Rule in Europe* (1944) applied the concept to the campaign of genocide that was underway in Poland and elsewhere in Nazi-occupied territories. Lemkin then campaigned to persuade the United Nations to draft a convention against genocide. The UN Convention on the Prevention and Punishment of the Crime of Genocide (1948), adopted after Lemkin's indefatigable lobbying, entrenched genocide in international and national laws for the first time. According to the Article 2 of the 1948 Convention, it is defined as 'any of the following acts committed with the intent to destroy in whole or in part a national, ethnical, racial or religious group':

- killing members of the group or deliberately inflicting on the group conditions of life calculated to bring about its physical destruction in whole or in part;
- causing serious bodily or mental harm to members of the group;
- imposing measures intended to prevent births within the group; and
- forcibly transferring children of the group to another group.

Article 3 describes as punishable the following acts: genocide, conspiracy to commit genocide, direct and public incitement to commit genocide, attempt to commit genocide, and complicity in genocide. The Convention placed a stronger emphasis than Lemkin on physical and biological destruction and less on broader social destruction. According to the Convention, one does not need to exterminate or seek to exterminate every member of a designated group. Actually, one does not need to kill anyone at all to commit genocide, although genocide unaccompanied by mass killing is rarely prosecuted. Between the 1950s and 1980s, the term 'genocide' languished almost unused by scholars; the explosion of public interest in genocide happened in the 1990s. Because some scholars consider the UN definition not all-encompassing and believe it omits several groups that arguably should have been included, more than twenty definitions of genocide (including the *Encyclopaedia of Genocide*, 1999) have been formulated through the last decades in an effort to complete, adjust, and even substitute the UN definition, which is still the international legal definition of genocide. The elements of these definitions may be divided into 'harder' and 'softer' positions. Harder positions are guided by concerns that genocide will be rendered banal or meaningless by careless use. Some ('The Uniqueness Thesis': Wiesel, 1976; Rosensaft, 1977) argue that such large usage will divert attention from the proclaimed uniqueness of the Holocaust. On the other hand, softer positions reflect concerns that excessively rigid framing (i.e. a focus on the total physical extermination of a group) rules out too many actions that demand to be included.

Among the recurrent elements present in genocide definitions, five main aspects may be identified: the agents, the victims, the goals, the scale, and the strategies. Most genocide scholars continue to emphasize the role of the State as the main agent of genocide, while accepting that in some cases, as with settler colonialism, non-State actors may play a prominent and at times dominant role. Among *agents*, there is a clear focus on State and official authorities in authors like Dandrian (1975), Horowitz (1976), Porter (1982), and Levene (2005) (cited in Jones, 2006). Other scholars (Thompson and

Quets, 1987; Chalk and Jonassohn, 1990; Fein, 1993; Shaw, 2007 cited in Jones, 2006) abjure the State-centric approach. The UN Convention, too, cites 'constitutionally responsible rules, public officials or private individuals among possible agents' (UN Convention on the Prevention and Punishment of Genocide, 1948 – Art. 4). *Victims* are routinely identified as social minorities. There is widespread assumption that victims must be civilians or non-combatants (Dandrian, 1975; Horowitz, 1976; Chalk and Jonassohn, 1990; Fein, 1993; Charny, 1994; Midlarsky, 2005; Sémelin, 2005; and Shaw, 2007 cited in Jones, 2006). The groups may be internally constituted and self-identified (i.e. group-as-such), as required by the Genocide Convention. However, from other perspectives, perpetrators may also define the target groups (Chalk and Jonassohn, 1990; Katz, 1994). Others, like Leo Kuper (1981), accept the UN Convention definition but regret the exclusion of political groups. The *goals* of genocide are the destruction/eradication of the victim group, whether this is defined in physical terms or includes 'cultural genocide'. Lemkin squarely designated genocidal 'objectives' as the disintegration of the political and social institutions of culture, language, national feelings, religion, and the economic existence of national groups. Shaw (2007) emphasizes the desire to destroy a collective's (generally a minority's) social power; Dandrian (1975) and Horowitz (1976) specify that genocide targets groups whose ultimate extermination is held to be 'desirable' and 'useful', and Horowitz asserts the State's desire to assure conformity and participation of the citizenry. Feierstein (2007) presented the concept of 'social death', intended as the destruction of social powers and existential identity as the essence of genocide; the elimination of the victim group aims at suppressing their identity by destroying the network of social relations that make identity possible at all, transforming the victims into 'nothing' and the survivors into 'nobodies'. The *scale* of a genocide varies from Katz's (1994) targeting of a victim group in 'its totality' and Sémelin's (2005) 'total eradication', to 'in whole or in large part' (Wallimann and Dobkwoski, 1987) and 'in whole or in part' (UN Convention, 1948; Harff, 2003). Horowitz (1976) emphasized the absolute dimension of 'mass murder'; others, on the other hand, maintain silence on the issue.

With genocidal *strategies*, Lemkin referred to a coordinated plan of different actions; for this reason, the UN Convention (1948) listed a range of such acts. Genocidal strategies may be direct or indirect as breaking the linkage between reproduction and socialization of children in the family or group of origin (Fein, 1993), including economic and biological subjugation (Wallimann and Dobkwoski, 1987). Furthermore, several scholars have attempted to devise a typology of genocide. Dandrian (1975), for example, distinguished five different types of genocide: cultural, latent, retributive, utilitarian, and optimal. Chalk and Jonassohn (1990) developed a typology based on the motive of the perpetrator, sustaining that the crime of genocide is usually committed as an attempt to eliminate a real or potential threat, spread terror among real or potential enemies, acquire economic wealth, or implement a belief, a theory, or an ideology. According to them, genocides varied by the types of society in which they occurred, the perpetrators, the victims, the groups, the accusations against them, and the results for the perpetrator society. Fein, in 1993, identified four types of genocide:ideological, retributive, developmental, and despotic. Charny (1994) distinguished six major types of genocide: genocidal massacre, which is mass murder on a smaller scale; intentional genocide, the explicit intention of destroying a specific targeted victim group; genocide in the course of colonization or consolidation of power; genocide in the course of aggressive or unjust war; war crimes against humanity; and genocide as a result of ecological destruction and abuse. Finally, Roger Smith (1999) classified five forms of genocide: redistributive, institutional, utilitarian, monopolistic, and ideological, which refers to the main motivation of carrying out mass murder. The different motivations for genocidal actions are the basis of all these models, as illustrated in Tables 2.1 and 2.2.

However, regardless of the strategy chosen, a consensus exists that genocide is committed with the intent to destroy (UN Convention, 1948), is structural and systematic (Horowitz, 1976), deliberate and organized (Wallimann and Dobkwoski, 1987), sustained (Harff, 2003), and constituted by a series of purposeful actions (Thomson and Quets, 1987; Fein, 1993). Moreover, there is something of a consensus that group 'destruction' must involve physical liquidation, generally in the form of mass killing (Horowitz, 1976; Fein 1993; Katz, 1994; Bloxham, 2009).

2.4 The issue of genocidal intent

Intent is actually one of the most important criteria in defining genocide. To claim genocide, the special intent of annihilating a particular group 'as such' must be shown. Some scholars argue that a charge of genocide should not even be considered if a specific intent could not be demonstrated (Jones, 2006). Intent can be both general and specific. The 'specific intent' implies a direct and manifest connection between act and outcome, whereas with 'general intent' the act and its genocidal consequences may be separated in geographical and temporal terms. This includes cases in which the perpetrators did not intend to harm others but should have realized or known that the behaviour made the harm likely. For instance, forcibly removing other members to reservations and then withholding food and medicine and kidnapping many of their children to raise as slaves outside of the group's culture clearly results in the destruction of that group of people, even if that

Table 2.1 Genocide definitions

AGENTS

State and Official Authorities	Non-State Actors
– Dandrian (1975)	– Thompson and Quetz (1987)
– Horowitz (1976)	– Chalk and Jonassohn (1990)
– Porter (1982)	– Fein (1993)
– Levene (2005)	– Shaw (2007)

VICTIMS

Civilians/Non-Combatants	Group 'as Such'	Group Defined by the Perpetrator	Political Groups
– Dandrian (1975)	Genocide Convention (1948)	– Chalk and Jonassohn (1990)	Kuper (1981)
– Horowitz (1976)		– Katz (1994)	
– Chalk and Jonassohn (1990)			
– Fein (1993)			
– Charny (1994)			
– Midlarsky (2005)			
– Sémelin (2005)			
– Shaw (2007)			

SCALE

Total	Whole or in large part	Whole or in part	Mass murder
– Katz (1994)	– Walliman and Bobkowski (1987)	– UN Convention (1948)	– Horowitz (1976)
– Sémelin (2005)		– Harff (2003)	

GOALS

– Lemkin (1944): disintegration of the political and social institution of culture, language, national feelings, religion, and the economic existence of national groups;
– Dandrian (1975), Horowitz (1976): destruction of groups whose ultimate extermination is held to be desirable and useful;
– Feierstein (2007): social death; and
– Shaw (2007): desire to destroy a minority's social power.

Table 2.2 Genocidal strategies and typology of genocide

GENOCIDAL STRATEGIES

Walliman and Dobkowski (1987): economic and biological subjugation; and Fein (1993): to break the linkage between reproduction and socialization of children in the family or group of origin.

TYPOLOGY OF GENOCIDE

Dandrian (1975):
- Cultural genocide
- Latent genocide
- Retributive genocide
- Utilitarian genocide
- Optimal genocide

Smith (1987):
- Redistributive genocide
- Institutional genocide
- Utilitarian genocide
- Monopolistic genocide
- Ideological genocide

Chalk and Jonassohn (1990): genocides vary by the types of society in which they occur, the perpetrators, the victims, the groups, the accusations against them, and the results for the perpetrator society.

Fein (1993):
- Ideological genocide
- Retributive genocide
- Developmental genocide
- Despotic genocide

---

result is neither intended or desired. It is difficult to show that the accused intended to destroy a substantial part of the group, but it arguably needs to be shown that the accused was in a position to destroy a substantial part of the group. It is also difficult to ascertain the state of mind of the perpetrators and planners in order to establish the intent to destroy a 'substantial' part of the group. The intent defines genocide. However, the intent is different from the *motive*. In international criminal law, motive is irrelevant. Prosecutors need only to prove that the criminal act was intentional, not accidental. In prosecution of genocide, tribunals have not required proof of a motive; in fact, the existence of a personal motive does not preclude the perpetrator from also having the specific intent to commit genocide. Establishing the *mens rea* (mental element) of genocidal intent poses significant challenges. How can one know what is in the perpetrator's mind? In the absence of a formal confession, intent must be inferred.

2.5 Prevention of genocide

Genocide addresses the question of how people perceive one another, and their behaviour when they try to interact. It conceives of humanity's future in light of how some people view themselves (superior, intelligent, vibrant, and perfectible), and to attain that future large numbers of so-called 'surplus humans' have been slaughtered (Rubenstein, 1983). Genocide does not emerge out of nothing. In all cases, there are always a number of preventable preliminary steps on the road to the 'ultimate solution' to the 'problem'. Such steps invariably involve processes of identification, alienation, isolation, and oppression, prior to the decisive stage of a target group's destruction (Bartrop, 2014). Prevention is usually mentioned as the single most important issue in genocide studies. As early as 1982, Charny proposed to create a genocide early warning system. Many academics insist that an adequate typology is crucial for preventing future genocides; scholars like Stanton, Huttenback, and Markausen believe that labelling one or another contemporary case of mass killing 'genocide' would help to end violence. However, as the case of Darfur, Sudan (in 2005) has shown, putting a name on a particular event does not automatically bring a solution to a problem. However, according to Staub (1999), distinguishing between genocide and mass killing is not especially useful from the standpoint of predicting and preventing collective violence or even understanding its origins. Because the word genocide has an emotional appeal, by identifying an event as genocide we unwittingly downgrade mass killing, which is abundant in the world today. Indeed, there is no international treaty on mass killing similar to the UN Genocide Convention (1948). It is practically impossible and functionally ineffective, for Staub, to focus on genocide prevention to the exclusion of all forms of mass violence.

2.6 Models of prevention

As outlined in Chapter 1, there are different models of assessing risks of genocide. Most of the scholars deal with three types of genocidal threats:

- possible mass atrocities/genocidal massacres/full-scale genocides of ethnic, national, religious, or political minorities by ruling elites in certain types of State;
- similar threats by one State against other States or groups within other States or State-like organisms; and
- similar threats by non-State actors in situations of civil war or unrest.

A fourth type is occasionally mentioned, but not really addressed. It concerns groups, whether based in a State or not, identifying with global genocidal ideologies attempting to conquer the world or large parts of it and advocating annihilation of opposing groups in the process (Bartoli, Bauer and Gurr, 2010). Some authors (Kressel, 1996; Rummel, 1996; Stanton, 1996) have written extensively about the underlying root conditions and causes of genocide and mass violence. Other authors (Hulsizer and Woolf, 2005) based their research on these authors' research, integrating and augmenting these theoretical models to create a risk analysis model aimed at the prevention of genocide. According to these scholars, the spiralling risk of fomenting enmity within a group directed against those defined as 'other' can be assessed by examining the factors underlying mass violence and genocide. Factors including group cultural history, situational factors, social psychological factors and context, and interpersonal factors can be examined to provide an assessment of risk for movement along a path of mass violence with hallmarks including stigmatization, dehumanization, moral disengagement, moral exclusion, impunity, and bystander interactions (Hulsizer and Woolf, 2005). Risk assessment can then be applied to an analysis aimed at the selection of effective prevention strategies. According to Staub (1999), difficult life conditions give rise to scapegoating and ideologies that identify enemies and lead one group to turn against another. Conflict between groups and self-interest are additional instigators of group violence. Discrimination and limited violence change individuals and groups and can lead to an evolution that ends in mass killing or genocide. Certain cultural characteristics make this process more likely. The passivity of bystanders allows it to unfold. To halt violence once it begins, action by nations and the community of nations is essential. Preventing group violence may require the healing of wounds due to past victimization, reconciliation, and the resolution of conflict between antagonistic groups.

Changes in elements of a group's culture are also important. Without prevention, great social changes and other contemporary conditions make frequent future group violence probable. The more the basic physical and psychological needs of groups of people are satisfied by constructive means, the less likely it is that psychological and social processes that lead to group violence arise. However, without significant efforts at prevention, group violence is likely to become more widespread. There are a number of reasons for this. In our interconnected world, as people see the riches that others possess, feelings of deprivation and injustice are likely to arise, and people turn to their group as a vehicle for improving their lives. In a world that is changing with tremendous speed, with small, local communities often destroyed, people turn to ethnic, religious, or ideological groups for security, identity, connection, and support. In a world where increasingly relatively small groups become new countries, the disengagement from and continuing conflict with the group they leave and conflicts around ethnicity and other subgroup differences in the new country are potential sources of violence (Staub, 1999). Adler et al., (2004) tried to develop an approach to the primary prevention of genocide, based on established public health-based violence prevention methods derived from a variety of high-risk settings. The principal findings of their research showed that mortality rates due to genocidal violence are far in excess of other public health emergencies including malaria and HIV/AIDS. The immediate and long-range health consequences of genocide include infectious diseases, organ system failure, and psychiatric disorders, conferring an increased burden of disease on affected populations for multiple subsequent generations. According to these scholars, structural risk factors for genocide within societies include totalitarian government, exclusionary ideologies, armed conflict, economic hardship, and inaction of bystander nations. Proposed psychological risk factors for genocidal behaviour include moral exclusion, authority orientation, action in self-interest, desensitization, and compartmentalized thinking. Their conclusion is that violence and injury prevention models, incorporating what is currently known about the societal and behavioural risk factors for genocide in high-risk populations, may be modified to address the primary prevention of catastrophic violence on a population-wide scale.

A number of existent global peace-building initiatives may serve as models for the design of future prevention initiatives in high-risk, pre-genocide jurisdictions. Because genocide is one of the most pressing threats to the health of populations in the twenty-first century, they suggest that recent advances in the public health discipline of violence prevention might provide a blueprint for approaches to primary genocide prevention based on epidemiological methods. The fragility of most States involved in genocide compound the conflict risks. For this reason, Marshall and Cole (2009) developed an index of State fragility and applied it globally to information on fourteen aspects of a State's capacity to deal with political challenges, maintain legitimacy, and deliver economic and social goods to its citizens. Joseph Hewitt (2010) identified five risk variables: major instability events, high infant mortality (signifying widespread poverty and lack of social services), high levels of militarization (indicating a readiness to use coercion against internal opposition), low levels of economic integration into the global economy (signifying both poverty and a lack of external economic influence that might mitigate political conflict), and a lack of regional security with one or more neighbouring countries involved in armed conflict, domestic or international. According to him, global empirical research showed these conditions to be precursors of instability in the recent past (Gurr, 2010). However, whereas systematic risk assessment is better than what we had before, it is not enough to indicate more precisely when genocidal violence is likely to begin.

High-risk profiles tell us when a country is in the latter stages of upheaval that may result in genocide. This alone should be enough to focus on preventing escalation. According to Yehuda Bauer (2010), non-military tools for prevention of all types of threats must necessarily be based in an analysis of power relations. Historical precedents may provide some clues and with globalization, it becomes possible (Bauer, 2010). This approach for assessing risks of future atrocities aims at identifying risks of future instability in a given region. It may not be possible to forecast risks of mass killings or repression, but it is possible to say what the chances are that any given State will experience, in their common precondition, violent instability in the near future. The models for genocide prevention used for this research are Stanton's Genocide Watch and Harff and Gurr's Country Risks of Genocide and Politicide Index Score. According to Stanton, genocide is a process that develops in ten stages that are predictable but not inexorable. At each stage, preventive measures can stop it. The process is not linear. Stages may occur simultaneously. Logically, earlier stages must precede later stages, but all stages operate throughout the process. The ten stages are classification, symbolization, discrimination, dehumanization, organization, polarization, preparation, persecution, extermination, and denial (Genocide Watch, 2013). Harff identified a model to assess risks of genocide. Her structural model identified the causal factors that jointly differentiate with 74% in 2003 (nearly 90% today) the thirty-six serious civil conflicts that led to episodes of genocidal violence between 1995 and 2002 and 93 others that did not (Harff, 2012).

Case studies will be presented in the next chapter.

Note

1 Marshall and Ramsey (1999), using the composite measure of gender empowerment, support these findings.

3   Case studies

This chapter presents the case studies, giving a general overview and analysing gender equality in these countries. This research aims at discovering what impact gender equality has on genocide. The main hypothesis is that the lower the gender equality, the greater the likelihood that a State will experience genocide. Beyond theoretical inquiry, this project calculates the covariance, the standard deviation for gender equality and genocide, and the Bravais-Pearson correlation coefficient to test the preceding hypothesis, taking Nigeria, Ethiopia, Angola, Burundi, and Uganda in 2009 as case studies. Given the limited temporal/space domain, caution about the generalizability of any findings is warranted. This research analyses the overall gender equality in these five countries through the data of the Global Gender Gap (GGG) Report 2009 from the World Economic Forum and through the OECD's (Organization for Economic Cooperation and Development) Social Institutions and Gender Index (SIGI). Starting from Harff and Gurr's Country Risks of Genocide and Politicide Index Score (2009), I use gender equality to try to understand why, with similar scores, some countries experienced genocide while others did not. The main goal is to test whether there is a correlation between gender equality and genocide, so as to consider adding gender indicators to the genocide prevention models and early warning mechanisms concerning the Responsibility to Protect. The presence/absence of genocide is tested with Genocide Alert from Gregory Stanton's Genocide Watch. The methodology of the research is explained in detail in Chapter 4.

3.1 Nigeria

Nigeria is the most populous country in Africa. The country is divided along religious, ethnic, and socio-economic fault lines, which split the country into a poor and predominantly Muslim north and a rich and predominantly Christian south. The military has ruled Nigeria for much of its history since independence from Britain in 1960 (Freedom House, 2009d). Beginning with the first military coup in 1966, military officers have claimed that their intervention was necessary to control simmering tensions among the country's 250 ethnic groups, as well as between religious communities (Freedom House, 2009d). The former British colony is one of the world's largest oil producers, but few Nigerians, including those in oil producing areas, have benefited. During the civil war (Nigerian-Biafran war in 1967–1969), over a million Ibos died because the federal government blocked international aid and basic foodstuffs, leading to the deaths of hundreds of thousands of civilians (Genocide Prevention Advisory Network [GPANET], 2012). This conflict originated from secessionist claims by Ojukwu, the Ibo leader, and other peoples in the oil-rich Niger Delta region, to declare the independence of the Republic of Biafra. Only Cote D'Ivoire, Gabon, and a few other States recognized Biafra. The Nigerian Army encircled Biafra and starved it into submission (Genocide Watch, 2012d). After lurching from one military coup to another, Nigeria finally got an elected leadership in 1999.

The southeast region is still restive and there are insurgencies among Niger Delta groups. Despite repeated efforts to install democratic institutions in Nigeria, ethnic-based tensions, endemic corruption, and the political ambitions of the military worked to weaken the fragile mandate of civilian rulers. The government still faces the growing challenge of preventing Africa's most populous country from breaking apart along ethnic and religious lines. Thousands of people have died over the past few years in communal attacks led by the Islamic State-aligned Boko Haram (BBC News, 2016d). Separatist aspirations have also been growing and the imposition of Islamic law in several northern States of Nigeria has embedded divisions and caused thousands of Christians to flee (BBC News, 2016d). There are several minorities at risk (i.e. Ibo, Ijaw, Ogoni, Yoruba, Hausa Muslim, and Christians in the north). Currently, Genocide Watch has declared a stage nine (extermination) to define the genocide stage in Nigeria. In fact, since the resurgence of Boko Haram in 2010, it has perpetrated many genocidal massacres against the civilian population. It presents a severe threat to the stability of Nigeria. Boko Haram targets people based on their ethnicity and religion and its declared goal is eradication of Christian and western influence in Nigeria: an exclusionary ideology characteristic of a genocidal group (Genocide Watch, 2012d). Its methodology is terror and mass murder. Boko Haram (literally translated, 'Western Education is Sin') is a criminal movement led by an Islamic extremist, Abubakar Shekau, who has vowed to destroy every Christian school in Nigeria and to carry out terrorist attacks on Nigerian police and government officials (Genocide Watch, 2014). The attacks aim at polarizing relations between the Muslim north and the

Christian south of Nigeria and have killed hundreds of people with Boko Haram proudly claiming 'credit' for these mass murders. Boko Haram has kidnapped hundreds of children from villages and boarding schools (Genocide Watch, 2014). Many of the kidnapped girls have been brutally ripped from their families and are used as sex slaves, housekeepers, and 'wives' for Boko Haram fighters, and most recently as suicide bombers. Kidnapped boys are often forced to fight for Boko Haram as child soldiers. To make the boys loyal to Boko Haram, many have been forced to kill their own families, leaving the children with no home to come back to (Genocide Watch, 2014). In addition to its terrible crimes against children, Boko Haram has been raiding and capturing villages and murdering their people. Since 2010, Boko Haram has killed thousands of civilians. The situation in Nigeria is critical.

3.2 Ethiopia

Ethiopia is the oldest independent country in Africa and, with a population of over 80 million people, it is the second most populous country in sub-Saharan Africa. Ethiopia is one of the world's poorest countries with a per capita income of only $1,000 (2010) per year (Genocide Watch, 2012). The country has a turbulent history of famine, drought, civil conflict, and war. Drought, famine, war, and ill-conceived policies brought millions to the brink of starvation in the 1970s and 1980s (BBC News, 2016c). Even if it claims to be an electoral democracy, in practice it is an authoritarian State (Genocide Watch, 2012c). It is plagued by decades of oppression, corruption, human rights violations, and sustained repression of opposition to its government. Authoritarian government and the exploitative economic system negate the principles of a democracy. Politics in Ethiopia is often defined by a power struggle between the Amharic and Tigrayan ethnic groups. The Ethiopian People's Revolutionary Democratic Front (EPRDF) is led by Tigrayans, and completely dominates Ethiopian politics. Political repression is rampant and the government uses development aid as a means to suppress political opposition and to oppress neglected minorities (Genocide Watch, 2012f). Genocide Watch declared a 'Genocide Emergency' in 2003, after massacres in Ethiopia's far southwestern region of Gambella. EPRDF militias initiated a systematic genocidal campaign targeting the indigenous Anuak people of Gambella province. Even though it lacks roads, electricity, and other basic infrastructures, and suffers from long-term political, social, and economic marginalization, the Gambella region has rich resources and fertile land (Genocide Watch, 2012f). The Ethiopian government's appetite for large-scale agricultural development is causing catastrophic damage to the social structure and land of the people of Gambella (Genocide Watch, 2012h).

The people have been forcibly driven off their land, and the land is being leased to Chinese, Saudi, and Indian multinational agrocorporations at rock-bottom prices. None of the money for the leased land is being used to benefit the people of Gambella. Over the last decade, the Anuak have pressed the government for income from their resources; in response, the government has initiated a genocidal campaign aimed at deporting, persecuting, and killing the Anuak people. In Gambella, tens of thousands of people have been forcibly relocated from their land (Genocide Watch, 2012h). In 2010, the Ethiopian government initiated a 'villagization' program. The programme intended to group scattered farming communities into small villages, with the aim of changing their lifestyle and providing better access to food, education, and health. However, the government's plans are far from reaching these goals; the Ethiopian government has forcibly relocated approximately 70,000 people from their land with the intention to lease the land for foreign and domestic investment (Genocide Watch, 2012h). There have been numerous reports of human rights violations (Genocide Watch, 2012h). Many of the new villages where people are being relocated have inadequate food and lack healthcare and educational facilities (Genocide Watch, 2012f). The Ethiopian government is detrimental to the livelihood of the people of Gambella. The government's failure to provide food assistance has caused endemic hunger and cases of starvation. In addition, those who have resisted relocating are repeatedly assaulted and arbitrarily arrested (Genocide Watch, 2012h).

In 2007, the Ethiopian government initiated a genocidal campaign against the Ogadeni civilian population (Genocide Watch, 2012g). The Ogaden region is endowed with rich oil and gas resources, but its population lives in extreme poverty while Chinese oil companies pump the oil and gas from under their land. Without the knowledge and consent of the Ogadeni, the Ethiopian government signed contracts and gave concessions to foreign oil companies to exploit and extract oil and natural gas from the Ogaden (Genocide Watch, 2012g). Immediately after oil and gas was discovered in the Ogaden, Ethiopian government forces evicted large numbers of Ogadenis from their land and herded them into internally displaced person (IDP) camps, causing a humanitarian disaster. Ten of thousands of people have also fled to refugee camps in Kenya and Somalia. Thousands of once self-sufficient Ogadenis have starved to death (Genocide Watch, 2012g). The Ethiopian government's policy in the Ogaden is to suppress all demands for autonomy from Ogadenis. It has included gradual starvation of the population in IDP camps (genocide by attrition) by cutting off the IDP camps from humanitarian aid (Genocide Watch, 2012g). The army has imposed an economic blockade on many towns and villages in the Ogaden. The government has restricted access to water, food, and other necessities. Food is being used as a weapon of war (Genocide Watch, 2012g). Massacres, torture, rape, and disappearance are prevalent in the Ogaden region. According to the International Displacement Monitoring Centre (IDMC), whole Ogadeni communities have been forcibly relocated to areas controlled by the army. Villagers and nomads were given a few days' notice to vacate their land. The Ogaden has been transformed into a vast military-occupied area with thousands of Ogadenis in IDP camps (Genocide Watch, 2012g). Given the situation in the country, Genocide Watch has declared stage nine of genocide, i.e. extermination, in Ethiopia.

3.3 Angola

One of Africa's major oil producers, Angola is striving to tackle the physical, social, and political legacy of a twenty-seven-year civil war that ravaged the country after independence from Portugal in 1975. The war was primarily led by the People's Movement for the Liberation of Angola (MPLA) and the National Union for the Total Independence of Angola (UNITA). After sixteen years of fighting, a fragile peace accord led elections. However, the leader of UNITA, Jonas Savimbi, rejected the outcome of these elections and resumed the conflict. In 1994, the war was broken up by another fragile period of peace. A peace accord was signed and UN peacekeepers were sent. However, this peacekeeping mission failed and the war continued until 2002, when Savimbi died. The death of UNITA's leader finally brought peace but, by that time, an estimated 500,000 people had been already killed. With the normalization of life in the country, new educational infrastructures such as schools and professional training centres have been built (BBC News, 2016a). The war produced over four million internally displaced persons and more than 300,000 refugees in neighbouring countries (80% of whom are women and children) (BBC News, 2016a). In addition, many resettled people, particularly those in the peripheral provinces, remained without land, proper shelter and food, healthcare, jobs, education, or even identification documents. The resettlement process was slowed by the presence of an estimated 500,000 landmines along with war-ruined infrastructure, which continued to make large tracts of the country inaccessible to humanitarian aid (Freedom House, 2009a).

Along with the conflict between UNITA and MPLA, a separatist struggle by the Front for the Liberation of Enclave of Cabinda (FLEC), which fought for the independence of Cabinda, also played a role in the civil war. The government has been fighting secessionists in the northern enclave of Cabinda intermittently since 1975. When Cabinda became part of Angola in 1975, the Cabindans were not consulted. Although the Angolan war ended in 2002, the status of Cabinda is still disputed by FLEC. A 2006 peace agreement between the government of Angola and a faction of FLEC sought to end the conflict, but sporadic attacks by both sides have continued. According to some sources, the refusal of the Angolan government to accept Cabindan claims for independence can largely be explained by the oil wealth in Cabinda, which accounts for 60% of Angola's oil production (Freedom House, 2009a). The government has sent thousands of troops to subdue the rebellion in the enclave, and human rights groups have alleged abuses against civilians. In a 2009 report, Human Rights Watch showed a disturbing pattern of human rights violations by the Angolan Army. Between September 2007 and March 2009, at least thirty-eight people were unlawfully arrested and accused of State security crimes. Many of these people were tortured (Genocide Watch, 2012a). Because of the deep-rooted conflict about Cabinda, in 2009 Genocide Watch considered the country at stage six of genocide, i.e. polarization.

3.4 Uganda

The Republic of Uganda is divided along ethnic and linguistic lines, with Bantu groups occupying the southeast region and the Acholi-Nilotic groups in the north. In Uganda, this ethnic divide has resulted in two recent genocides. In 1962, Uganda gained its independence from the British and joined the British Commonwealth. Following independence, in 1966 Milton Obote, leader of the Uganda People's Congress (UPC), became president without an official election. In 1971, Obote was overthrown in a military coup led by his army chief of staff, Idi Amin Dada. Amin was a bloody dictator who ordered the deaths of between 100,000 and 300,000 people during his eight-year rule (Genocide Watch, 2012e). He targeted all his political enemies and the Acholi and Langi groups. His dictatorship came to an end in 1979 when Uganda invaded Tanzania, and Tanzania responded by overthrowing Amin. After a one-year interim, elections returned Milton Obote to power as president. Obote began another genocide against the Baganda people and laid waste to the Luwero Triangle north of Kampala. Yuweri Museveni's National Resistance Army began its campaign to take over Uganda, and during the civil war, an estimated 300,000 more Ugandans lost their lives (Genocide Watch, 2012). Obote was overthrown in July 1985 by Acholi troops and fled into exile in Zambia. Such acts of violence led to the formation of rebel groups such as the Lord's Resistance Army (LRA). This group is guilty of brutal crimes against humanity including mass murder, displacement of a million people, recruitment of child soldiers, child sex slavery, and other crimes (Genocide Watch, 2012e). In 1995, the LRA launched an attack in Atiau resulting in mass atrocities on villagers, killing and abducting hundreds of people. The following year, LRA kidnapped 139 school girls and made them sex slaves. According to UNICEF data, the LRA has abducted at least 25,000 children since the conflict began. According to the UN Office for the Coordination of Humanitarian Affairs (US Agency for International Development [USAID], 2006), the LRA attacks and the government's counter-insurgency measures have resulted in the displacement of nearly 95% of the Acholi population in three districts of northern Uganda. By 2006, 1.7 million people lived in more than 200 internally displaced person camps in northern Uganda (USAID, 2006). These camps had some of the highest mortality rates in the world. The Ugandan Ministry of Health and partners (2005) estimated that through the first seven months of 2005, about 1,000 people were dying weekly, chiefly from malaria and AIDS, and violence accounted for 9.4% of the deaths, occurring mostly outside the camps. The people killed were mostly adult males (70,1%) but 16.9% were children under fifteen years. It is estimated that 3,971 people were killed in the studied population between January and July 2005 (The Republic of Uganda, Ministry of Health, 2005). In 2006–2008, a series of meetings were held in Juba, Sudan, between the government of Uganda and the LRA, mediated by the South Sudanese separatist leader Riek Machar. The Ugandan government and the LRA signed a truce on 26 August 2006. Under the terms of the agreement, LRA forces would leave Uganda and gather in two assembly areas in the remote Garamba National Park area of northern Democratic Republic of Congo that the Ugandan government agreed not to attack. In December 2008–March 2009, however, the armed forces of Uganda, the DRC, and South Sudan launched aerial attacks and raids on the LRA camps in Garamba, destroying them, but the efforts to inflict a final military defeat on the LRA were not fully successful. Rather, they provoked brutal revenge attacks by scattered LRA remnants, with over 1,000 people killed and hundreds abducted in Congo and South Sudan, and hundreds of thousands displaced while fleeing the massacres. Moreover, the military action in the DRC did not result in the capture or killing of Joseph Kony, the leader of LRA, who remained elusive (BBC News, 2009). In 2009, concerns still remained about serious human rights violations related to the unresolved conflict between LRA rebels and the military. Genocide Watch declared stage six, i.e. polarization.

3.5 Burundi

Since its independence from Belgium in 1962, Burundi has been confronted with ethnic violence between the Hutu majority and Tutsi minority. The minority Tutsi ethnic group governed Burundi for most of the period following independence. The judiciary, military, business sector, news media, and educational system have also traditionally been dominated by the Tutsi. Violence between them and the majority Hutu has broken out repeatedly since independence. Between 1959 and 1963 an estimated 50,000 Hutus were killed by the Tutsi government (Genocide Watch, 2012b). In 1972, the Tutsi army murdered an estimated 150,000 Hutus including nearly all educated Hutus in attempt to 'decapitate' the Hutu leadership. In 1988, another 25,000 Hutus were killed at Ntega and Maranga in northern Burundi (Genocide Watch, 2012b). Peace talks led by Burundi President Buyoya resulted in the first multi-party elections in Burundi. However in 1993, Ndadaye (the first Hutu president in the country) was murdered (Genocide Watch, 2012b). His assassination set off a twelve-year civil war, marked by a downward spiral of revenge killings that produced a 'bilateral genocide' by the two dominant groups against each other (Genocide Watch, 2012b). This bilateral genocide killed an estimated 300,000 people in Burundi, mostly civilians. Negotiations on power sharing took place over the succeeding months, as ethnic violence continued to plague the country. Ndadaye's successor was killed in 1994, along with Rwandan President Juvenal Habyarimana, when their plane was apparently shot down as it approached Kigali airport in Rwanda. This event triggered the Rwandan genocide and intensified the violence in Burundi. Even under the new Hutu president, Sylvester Ntibantunganya, peace and political stability within the country continued to be elusive as armed insurgents sporadically staged attacks and government forces pursued an often-ruthless campaign of intimidation. The situation somewhat stabilized with the organization of the 2005 elections. In the spring of 2008, violence exploded again between government soldiers and the last active rebel group, the National Liberation Forces (FNL), which operated in territory near the capital. In May 2008 the government and the FNL signed a ceasefire agreement. In April 2009, the FNL laid down its arms and officially transformed into a political party in a ceremony supervised by the African Union. Genocide Watch has declared a Genocide Alert, considering Burundi at stage seven, i.e. preparation. While the current conflict is primarily political in nature, there is risk of it reigniting pre-existing ethnic cleavages. In fact, civil unrest erupted in Burundi in 2015, following the 26th of April announcement by the ruling party, the National Council for the Defense of Democracy–Forces for the Defense of Democracy (CNDD-FDD), that President Pierre Nkurunziza would run for a third term in 2015 elections. Opposition parties in Burundi claimed that this was a direct violation of the Arusha Peace Agreement and Burundi Constitution, which limits presidents to two terms in office. There were reports that hate speech and incitement to violence by the government were increasing. Both Amnesty International and the UN Security Council expressed grave concern regarding violations of right to life, inhumane and degrading treatment, arbitrary arrests and detention, and violation of press freedom and the right to information. Members of the 'Imbonerakure', the youth wing of the CNDD-FDD, committed human rights abuses on the pretext of maintaining security. They prevented opposition party meetings, and intimidated, attacked, and killed members of the opposition with impunity. According to the United Nations High Commissioner for Refugees over 158,000 Burundians have fled the country since 13 April 2015 (Genocide Watch, 2015).

3.6 Overall gender equality

'Violence against women' includes any act of gender-based violence that results in physical, sexual, or psychological harm or suffering to women including threats of such acts, coercion, or arbitrary deprivation of liberty, whether occurring in public or private life, such as systematic rape (Jekayinfa, 2007). Violence against women affects many women and girls. Particularly vulnerable are women living in extremely precarious conditions (i.e. those who are discriminated because of race, language, ethnic group, religion, handicap, or membership of a minority group, indigenous, and displaced women). Physical, sexual, and psychological violence against women between a couple and in the family consists of battery, marital rape, dowry-related violence, incest, or spousal violence. Violence occurring within the community includes sexual harassment, rape, and sexual assault, intimidation at work, forced treatment, abusive medication, and the exploitation and commercialization of women's bodies. Violence against women also includes contraception imposed by constraint, forced sterilization or abortions, selective abortion of female foetuses, and female infanticide (Jekayinfa, 2007). Discrimination against women is especially problematic in northern African States governed by Sharia statutes, where women's rights have suffered particularly serious setbacks. There is high oppression of women and continued female relegation to an inferior status (Agbiboa and Maiangwa, 2014).

African women in general and Nigerian women in particular are submerged in extreme poverty; they are victims of all kinds of abuse, discrimination, and exploitation. The vulnerability of women and girls in northern Nigeria to radical elements and criminals is partly due to religious convictions/laws, cultural traditions, and the socio-economic status of women in the region. Powerful cultural traditions and rigid interpretations of Islam interact to produce a pattern of gender stratification so extreme as to virtually imprison the entire female population in northern Nigeria (Diamond, 1987).

It is common to find young girls in northern Nigeria hawking petty goods in the streets, or married off to men at a very young age.

Ethiopian culture is also based on patriarchal traditions and beliefs. Religious leaders hold great influence over public opinion and usually advocate extreme patriarchal and discriminatory attitudes. When women speak about the violation of their rights, they are told they are becoming 'westernized', even by men who are educated (Berhane, 2005). In Ethiopia, discrimination against women is perpetuated by customary traditions of abduction and rape, always followed by early marriage, seen as the norm in some parts of Ethiopian society.

In Angola, during the civil war that ensued after independence, Angolan women experienced sexual violence and rape at the hands of soldiers and rebels, were identified as 'witches' and burned at the stake, forced to do manual labour, and used as 'couriers'. Before the peace accord, there were reports of governmental forces attacking women in their homes, while they worked in the fields, and near military camps. A study conducted by the United Nations Population Fund (UNFPA) in 2000 reported that out of 1,400 internally displaced persons interviewed, 20% reported knowing of women who had been raped, and 38% of women had been abused by their husbands or intimate partners (ACGSD, 2010). Women who were abducted by the rebel group UNITA faced the dilemma of whether or not to leave their UNITA husbands and return to their original homes, where they risked being rejected. The war and its impacts increased women's workloads, as they took on a greater responsibility for activities usually performed by men, such as building and repairing houses, providing for the household, disciplining male children, fulfilling religious and social obligations, and dealing with community leaders and government officials (Ducados, 2004). Many continue to perform these tasks even in peacetime, mainly because their husbands have died or deserted the household. According to the African Development Bank (2008), the loss or displacement of men associated with decades of conflict has led to an increase in female-headed households in Angola. The 2006–2007 Angola Malaria Indicator Survey found that 25% of households were headed by women. Although women's increasing economic role has challenged traditional stereotypes of the role of women in the family, the end result for many women has been work overload in an effort to combine economic activity and household duties. Moreover, the African Development Bank (2008) reports that female-headed households are subject to discriminatory treatment, i.e. female-headed households are provided with minimal support from the government. Women's life in Angola is also characterized by high levels of maternal and child mortality, poverty, violence, malnutrition, illiteracy, lack of resources, unemployment in the formal sectors, and a high rate of participation in the informal economy. The strong persistence of patriarchal attitudes and deep-rooted stereotypes regarding the roles and responsibilities of women are discriminatory toward women. Entrenched cultural norms relegate women and girls to the area of domestic affairs only.

In Uganda, many women and girls suffer from sexual and gender-based violence committed by State actors, military services, and rebel armies, as well as non-State actors within the family and the community (ACGSD, 2010). The persistence of patriarchal patterns of behaviour and the existence of stereotypes relating to the role of women perpetuate the discrimination of women within Ugandan society (Amnesty International, 2007). The difficulties women face are not only due to intimidation, hostility, and ridicule from the community, but also due to the State's inaction in ensuring redress (Amnesty International, 2007).

Finally, 90% of the population of Burundi live in rural areas in widespread poverty. Women are particularly vulnerable to these economic problems because of the persistence of deeply entrenched patriarchal and stereotypical behaviour on women's roles and responsibilities. The general poverty in which women (especially rural and older women) live limits their access to adequate education, health services, social security, and land and banking services.

3.7 Physical integrity

3.7.1 Nigeria

In Nigeria, domestic violence and rape continue to affect women, and the practice of female genital mutilation and child marriage are pervasive. The term 'female genital mutilation' (FGM) applies to a range of practices involving the removal of all or parts of the clitoris and other external genitalia. In its most severe form it is known as 'infibulation' in which both the clitoris and both labia are removed and the two sides of the vulva are sewn together, leaving only a small opening to allow urine and menstrual period to pass (Bazza, 2010). Usually, these mutilations are executed with blunt and nonsterile instruments in very unhygienic circumstances. The mystical reasons behind the harmful practice are that it prevents promiscuity in women, controls female sexuality, and preserves the virginity of young girls until marriage. The 2008 DHS (Demographic and Health Survey) reports that nearly 30% of women aged fifteen to forty-nine years have experienced FGM. Out of 130 million 'circumcised' women in the world, a great percentage are Nigerians (Bazza, 2010).

'Early marriage' is the act of giving out a female child for marriage at a very tender age. In Nigeria, as in other parts of Africa, early marriage comes

in the form of child betrothal; this involves marrying out a girl child immediately after she is delivered. In other cases, the girls are withdrawn from
school or even denied access to education. There are cases in which parents
have forced their grown daughters into marriages against their wishes either
due to cultural, social, economic, or political reasons. As Nigeria is a federal
republic, each state has the authority to draft its own legislation. The Child
Rights Act of 2003 amended the Constitution to set the minimum age of
marriage at eighteen for both sexes, but only twenty-four of Nigeria's thirty-
six states have adopted the act. As a result, state laws on the minimum age
of marriage vary: in southern Nigeria, the minimum legal age of marriage
is between eighteen and twenty-one years of age, depending on the region;
in the north it ranges from twelve to fifteen years. The DHS estimated that
in 2008, 28.4% of girls between fifteen and nineteen years were married,
separated, divorced, or widowed.

Despite the existence of laws against rape, domestic violence, female
mutilation, and child marriages, there have been low rates of reporting and
prosecution of these offences. No national laws criminalize domestic violence. In addition, Nigeria's Penal Code grants husbands permission to beat
their wives, provided the violence does not result in serious injury (Organization for Economic Cooperation and Development [OECD], 2014d).
Domestic violence remains widespread and is somewhat considered socially
acceptable. According to the 2008 DHS, over 30.5% of women who have
ever been married have experienced some form of physical, sexual, or emotional violence at some point, and 18% of women reported experiencing
intimate physical or sexual violence in their lifetime. Domestic violence
affects women in Nigeria irrespective of age, class, educational level, and
place of residence. Records have it that violence within families in Nigeria
has reached alarming proportions. Reports of beatings, torture, acid attacks,
and killing of women in families or relationships are regular features in the
media and documented reports (Bazza, 2010). Shija (2004) reported that
in Nigeria, an average of 300–350 women are killed every year by their
husbands, former partners, boyfriends, or male relations. Most times, the
incidences are considered 'family feuds', which should be treated within
the family. Most police refuse to intervene and advise the victims to go back
home and settle 'family matters' (Bazza, 2010).

Rape incidence in Nigeria is increasing. In the country, 12–15% of
women have been forced by an intimate partner or ex-partner to have sex
at some time in their lives (Watt and Zimmerman, 2002). Rape is punishable with a fine and ten years to life imprisonment in Nigeria, but there
are no sanctions in the Penal Code against spousal rape. Societal pressure
to keep silent, victim-blaming, and stigmas surrounding sexual violence
mean that few women report sexual assaults. Although accurate figures as

to prevalence are unavailable, rape and sexual violence is recognized as a widespread, serious problem in Nigeria. There are accounts of the mass rape of female university students, with limited willingness of the police and university authorities to investigate, as well as the rape and sexual assault of women held in police custody. There is no law specifically addressing sexual harassment in Nigeria nor is sexual harassment addressed in other legislation. Sexual harassment is, however, considered to be widespread, and includes the practice of demanding sexual favours in return for employment or grades in university.

3.7.2 Ethiopia and Angola

Violence against women is a general problem in Ethiopia, where culturally based abuses, including wife beating and marital rape, are pervasive social problems with wide acceptance. A July 2005 World Bank study concluded that 88% of rural women and 69% of urban women believed their husbands had the right to beat them. While women have recourse via the police and courts, societal norms and limited infrastructure prevent many women from seeking legal redress, particularly in rural areas. The government prosecutes offenders only on a limited scale (African Centre for Gender and Social Development, [ACGSD], 2010). A survey conducted among 1,401 female students in high schools in Addis Ababa and Western Shoa in 1997 reported that the prevalence of completed rape and attempted rape against female students was 5% and 10%, respectively. The age range of those against whom rape was committed was between two and twenty-three years, and 85% of the victims were less than 18 years of age (Tadiwos, 2001). Marriage by abduction, which involves rape, is still very prevalent. According to surveys conducted by the National Committee on Traditional Practices of Ethiopia (NCTPE), the prevalence of marriage by abduction is 69% (ACGSD, 2010). Traditional practices endure within the rural communities where individual status is closely linked to family strength and success, and a daughter is expected to get successfully married in order to establish strategic kinships with other families. Domestic violence is also prevalent in Ethiopia and takes various forms of physical, sexual, and emotional abuse. Community-based studies indicate that 50–60% of women experience domestic violence in their lifetime. The study also concluded that sexual violence was more prevalent than physical violence, with the perpetrators mainly intimate partners and close family members (Berhane, 2005). Domestic violence is a crime under the Criminal Code, which under Art. 555–560 applies to a person who 'by doing violence to a marriage partner or a person cohabitating in an irregular union, causes grave or common injury to his/her physical or mental health' (OECD, 2014c). However, it is unclear what the punishment is for offenders, or how this law is implemented in practice. A 2009 study of the World Health Organization found that 70% of Ethiopian women suffered physical violence from their husband or partner at some point in their life, and over 50% had suffered physical violence in the preceding twelve months. Significant numbers of women experienced violence during pregnancy (Semahegn and Mengiste, 2015). The Penal Code establishes penalties for rape of between five and twenty years imprisonment.

As elsewhere, sexual violence, predominantly against women, was a feature of the conflict between Ethiopia and Eritrea in the 1990s and continues to be reported in the Ogaden region. According to Human Rights Watch, 'systematic' rape has been a feature of the government's counter-insurgency strategy in the region since 2007, directed against women suspected of having links to the Ogaden National Liberation Front. FGM is prevalent and reputable research indicates that more than 74.3% of Ethiopian women aged fifteen to forty-nine have been subjected to FGM (Alemu and Asnake, 2007). The vast majority of ethnic groups perform the practice when the girl is an infant. Less than one third of the women interviewed want the practice to be continued (Alemu and Asnake, 2007). Sexual harassment is not criminalized under the labor code in Ethiopia. Sex work is legal but the law prohibits pimping and benefiting from prostitution. Whosoever gains from the profession is punishable by imprisonment and a fine. Ethiopia is one of five countries making up over 50% of global maternal deaths (OECD, 2014c). Young motherhood is considered one of the main causes for Ethiopia's high levels of maternal mortality.

Contrarily, in Angola harmful traditional practices such as early marriages and female genital mutilation are rare and only occur in remote areas. However, domestic violence and sexual abuse against women and young girls is a daily reality for Angolan women. Violence against women in Angola is common and has been rising since the twenty-seven-year long civil war ended in 2002. In 2006, local human rights and women's organizations reported an increase in domestic and sexual violence against women and girls, including violence against girls in the school system. Women's experience of violence in Angola cannot be separated from the conflict and its ongoing consequences, including displacement and poverty. Although there is no data on prevalence, it is reported that many women in Angola were victims of rape and abduction during the war. Women with disabilities are especially prone to physical integrity violations (OECD, 2014a).

A significant amount of homicides are perpetrated against women, usually by their spouses (OECD, 2014a). The traditional view is that the woman is the guilty party and the man has a right to punish her. Family members often discourage victims from filing a complaint. Sexual violence extends to the school system where girls have been required to provide sexual favours in order to pass a grade (Human Rights Watch, 2007). Women remain reluctant to report violence due to the social stigma attached to it; women victims of rape remain silent for fear of not regaining social respect and not being able to find partners who would marry them. However, increased training on the rights of women and several high profile abuse cases have worked towards changing this view (OECD, 2014a).

3.7.3 Uganda

Research by the Coalition Against Gender Violence was done within two of Uganda's major districts; it was found that domestic violence was the most common form of violence in the community (67%) and wife beating was considered normal practice in accordance with cultural beliefs (26%) (The Coalition Against Gender Violence and UNFPA, 2004). According to the research, some ethnic groups believe that the practice of wife beating expresses physical affection and commitment to the relationship as well as instilling discipline (The Coalition Against Gender Violence and UNFPA, 2004). Sexual violence is a widespread problem in Uganda. 39% of women have experienced sexual violence compared to 11% of men, and 59.6% of women have experienced physical violence since age fifteen, compared to 53% of men. Violence occurs mostly in marriage. In fact, 62% of married women have experienced violence compared to 52% of never-married women (Action for Development Report, [ACFODE], 2009). Most perpetrators of physical violence in Uganda are family members and 50.4% of physical violence against women is committed by their current husband or partner. Sexual violence includes defilement, rape, incest, sexual harassment, marital rape, abortion, unwanted sexual touch, words, and putting mirrors between girls' legs. Other forms of sexual violence are use of bad/vulgar language, forced early marriages, sex with a woman during her postnatal period, words and signs related to sex, and attempted defilement, as well as indecent assault and sex in the presence of children. There are still cultural-related tendencies to regard some sexual violence offences, such as unwanted sexual touches and marital rape, as normal (ACFODE, 2009). Incidents of domestic violence and sexual abuse, including rape, often go unreported and are rarely investigated. Police lack the resources and capacity to investigate cases of rape.

Another problem that has been experienced in Uganda is that of gender-based violence in armed conflict situations. The conflict has been characterized by gender-based violence where mass rapes were common and women and girls were used as tools against the opposition. More than 32,000 children have been abducted to be used as child combatants and sex slaves (Amnesty International, 2007). Women, who are usually restricted to the home, were susceptible to rape, defilement, and other sexual abuses. Up to 27% of women have encountered rape during the armed conflict (The Coalition Against Gender Violence and UNFPA, 2004).

Cultural practices such as female genital mutilation have persisted even though in September 2009 the Ugandan government finalized a National Strategy for the Elimination of Female Genital Mutilation (ACGSD, 2010). Under the Constitution, the Children Act, and the Amendment to the Penal Code, the minimum legal age of marriage is eighteen years for men and women. However, despite the constitutional provision against early marriage, Uganda's marriage and family laws contradict this. Arranged marriages for minors still exist, especially in rural areas. The Coalition Against Gender Violence and UNFPA (2004) found that 11% of women are forced into marriage (ACGSD, 2010). The penal code provides that sex with a girl under eighteen is a felony and is punishable by life imprisonment (Amnesty International, 2007). Implementation is difficult to enforce as people's attitudes toward sexual activity is in variance to statutory law (The Coalition Against Gender Violence and UNFPA, 2004). However, sexual abuse of minors is increasing, according to the Ugandan Human Rights Commission (Freedom House, 2009e). Teenage pregnancy is significant in Uganda; associated reasons are social and economic, as well as linked to traditional practices and cultural norms. There is also the underlying assumption that a girl who has menstruated is ready to become pregnant and has reached adulthood (OECD, 2014e).

3.7.4 Burundi

It is estimated that 42% of women in Burundi have experienced some form of domestic violence (ACGSD, 2010). In 2008, a report to the Convention on the Elimination of All Forms of Discrimination against Women (CEDAW) Committee prepared by Burundian NGOs differentiated the violence experienced by women in different categories and at the hands of different actors. Within the family, gender-based violence takes the form of sexual violence (incest, marital rape, and sexual harassment); physical and verbal domestic violence; and economic violence. Within the community, physical and sexual violence (especially rape) is widespread; sexual harassment happens in the workplace, especially in the context of unregulated domestic work. The report also highlights State violence against women (i.e. violence committed by agents who abuse their position and authority), sexual violence, or other violations linked to the nonseparation of male and female detainees and the failure to provide adequate facilities and care as required by pregnant or breastfeeding women detainees; and arbitrary arrests and detentions following marital disputes or based on illegal grounds

(ACAT and OMET, 2008). In the absence of official statistics, the report submits data gathered by civil society. From 2004 to November 2007, the Seruka centre of Médecins Sans Frontières (MSF) Belgium registered 5,466 cases of sexual violence, an average of 1,366 victims per year and twenty-seven victims a week. In 2005, Iteka League and MSF Belgium reported 1,791 cases of sexual violence, an average of thirty-four victims a week. In 2006, they reported 1,930 cases of sexual violence, an average of thirty-seven victims a week. In the same year, a study by the gender unit of UNOB (UN Operation in Burundi) indicated that 60% of reported rapes involved children and 24% of the rape victims were less than eleven years old. The statistics only reflect reported cases. Many victims do not speak up for several reasons, especially the fear of reprisals. The report states that forms of violence other than those of a sexual nature are particularly underreported, as the victims of such violence will not benefit from free medical care (CEDAW, 2008).

Women's safety in Burundi has been significantly affected by conflict. Violence against women was particularly severe during the armed conflict and included rape, torture, and enslavement of young girls and women. During the war women experienced rape preceded or followed by brutality or cruel treatment; massacres and looting; forced enlistment and other consequential suffering; and forced displacement with difficulties in recovering rights after the conflict (especially property rights) (CEDAW, 2008). Moreover, NGOs have reported that the conflict has forced many women into prostitution. Even after the end of the war there have been reports that government and rebel soldiers raped women in the areas around Bujumbura after their withdrawal in 2001. It is reported that rebels abducted scores of women to provide domestic and sexual services in their camps (Choomaraswamyn, 2003). Due to forced removal by the Tutsi-dominated army, up to 80% of the population living around Bujumbura was relocated to reassembly camps throughout the province. The camps were sites of grave human rights violations where both government soldiers and rebel forces raped and brutalized the women who left the camps to find food and water (ACGSD, 2010). Since the ceasefire, it is reported that violence against women and children continues to increase (OECD, 2014b). The police and judicial authorities are doing little to respond to victims, or to find and punish those responsible. Because victims themselves are often shunned by relatives and their communities, women rarely disclose or report the crimes. Those who do seek help turn to medical aid and counselling services at international health centres, rather than going to the police (Zicherman, 2007). According to data, of 3,715 cases reported, just 823 have been investigated and among these just sixty cases have been prosecuted and fifty-three penalized (OECD, 2014b). Thus, despite the problem of endemic sexual violence receiving widespread attention (including a national plan to combat gender-based violence) there remain significant barriers to women seeking justice through the legal system. According to the African Development Bank, women victims of violence rarely report the incidents to the police especially in case of rape (OECD, 2014b). A report by the Global Network of Women Peacebuilders (2011) found that the underreporting of sexual and gender-based violence cases in Burundi is due to several factors (i.e. the lack of medical evidence due to lack of access to medical facilities, slowness of judicial facilities, and corruption in the justice system). The World Organization against Torture (2008) reports that sexual violence is generally trivialized in the community (as well as within the police and the judiciary) (ACAT and OMCT, 2008). As such, perpetrators enjoy a culture of impunity for their actions. Furthermore, the fear of stigmatization and reprisal also prevents women from reporting sexual violence (OECD, 2014b).

Domestic violence against women is reported to be common and on the rise since the ceasefire in 2002, and although population-based studies are also lacking in this area, domestic violence affects one in two women in Burundi, according to the African Development Bank (OECD, 2014b). Sexual harassment is also reported to be common in the family and in the community. Sexual harassment is criminalized in Art. 563 of Law. No. 1/05. The law prohibits sexual harassment, including the use of orders, severe pressure, or threats of physical and psychological violence to obtain sexual favours. The sentence for sexual harassment ranges from fines to penalties of one month to two years in prison. The sentence for sexual harassment doubles if the victim is less than eighteen years old. However, the government does not actively enforce this law. There are reports that sexual harassment occurs, but no data has been found on its frequency or extent (OECD, 2014b). There is no evidence that female genital mutilation is practiced (OECD, 2014b).

3.7.5 Human trafficking

Another phenomenon negatively affecting women in Africa is human trafficking.

Illegal human trafficking to, from, and within Nigeria for the purpose of forced labour and prostitution is reported to be increasing (Jekayinfa, 2007). According to the Women's Consortium of Nigeria, hundreds of Nigerian women and girls are trafficked each year into forced prostitution. They are made to endure slave-like conditions in foreign countries. Due to many factors including the escalating level of poverty, lack of viable opportunities, falling family values, the attraction to earn foreign exchange that is more valuable than the local currency, and the desire to get rich quickly, many parents use any means to force their children into the trafficking ring (ACG-DSD, 2010). According to a report of the US State Department, Ethiopia is also a source country for men, women, and children trafficked primarily for the purposes of forced labour and, to a lesser extent, for commercial sexual exploitation (ACGSD, 2010). Young women from all parts of Ethiopia are trafficked for domestic servitude, primarily to Lebanon, Saudi Arabia, and the United Arab Emirates, but also to Bahrain, Djibouti, Sudan, Syria, and Yemen. Djibouti, Egypt, and Somalia are reportedly the main transit routes for trafficked Ethiopians. Some women are trafficked into the sex trade after arriving at their destinations (ACGDSD, 2010).

Trafficking of women and children for domestic servitude has also increased in Angola, with victims being trafficked to neighbouring countries, such as the Democratic Republic of Congo, Namibia, and South Africa. Although there is no data on prevalence, trafficking for sexual exploitation is a problem both into and out of Angola (OECD, 2014a).

Trafficking and forced prostitution are also prevalent in Burundi and Uganda. The latter is a source and destination country for men, women, and children trafficked for the purposes of forced labour and sexual exploitation. Ugandan children are trafficked within the country, as well as to Canada, Egypt, the United Arab Emirates, and Saudi Arabia for forced labour and commercial sexual exploitation (US Department of State, 2008).

3.8 Education

Male preference over females is widely practiced in Nigeria, which robs the girl child of her rights to equal education. 'The male child is perceived as an asset, highly treasured in the family name because he will perpetrate the family' (Ezeliora and Ezeokana, 2011 p. 343). The female child is treated with disregard because she will be married out to another family, and if given education, she will in the future develop another man's home at the detriment of her biological home and is therefore seen as a waste of resources (Atama, 2012). This practice is the beginning of the exclusion of females from the social mainstream. They are marginalized and regarded as second-class citizens, incapable of developing their God-given potential as they are considered inferior and of low intelligence, incapable of making good and rational decisions for themselves and others and therefore are not expected to perform well in school (Atama, 2012). Poverty in a family discourages parents from educating their female children; rather some of the affected girls go on the streets, hawking petty goods in order to generate income to alleviate the family's financial problems. The resultant effect on some of these girls is prostitution, unwanted pregnancy, abortion, and ultimately death. In spite of the constitutional guarantees of equal access to education for all by the federal government of Nigeria, a nationwide campaign for the enrolment of all school-age children, and programs for adult and non-formal education, there are still traditional obstacles to female education and curricular insensitivity to gender and to civil and political rights. Many girls do not go to school because of the ignorance of their parents. They live in the remotest areas and have no access to western education. Moreover, some parents perceive that if they send their female children to school, girls will not keep good matrimonial homes. Nigerian society looks upon females who go to school as prostitutes, expensive to be maintained, proud, and in the end they may not have husbands to settle down with in their own homes (Kasin-Oghabor, 2005). Many men believe that education is not good for wives because they are in school together with men. Such misconceptions make it difficult for uneducated parents to send their female children to school and the vicious cycle continues. For these reasons – despite the continued efforts of government, individuals, groups, and organizations that aim to bring global understanding and commitment to women's increased access and participation as a necessary and indispensable condition for overall societal development – women still occupy very low scores in the educational indices of access and participation as well as performance. Of those interviewed for the 2008 Demographic and Health Survey (DHS), 30% of women aged twenty to twenty-four had received no education, compared to 13.7% of men in the same age bracket. Secondary school completion rates for women in this age bracket were 27.4% compared to 37.9% of men. This would indicate the preference towards a son in regard to access to education.

Similarly, 2008–2012 data from UNICEF (United Nations Children's Fund) indicates a gender gap to the detriment of girls in secondary and primary education in Ethiopia. Despite some progress, Ethiopia's education indicators are still poor and below sub-Saharan averages. As it is evident from the statistics, Ethiopian boys have more access to education than Ethiopian girls (UN Educational, Scientific and Cultural Organization [UNESCO], 2011). The great disparity can be found in secondary education and adult literacy. For every 100 boys enrolled in secondary education, there are approximately only seventy-seven girls. The number of female drop-outs is high in the country, especially in the transition from primary to secondary education. In 2009, only 41% of girls survived to the last grade of primary education and there were only 30% enrolled in secondary education. Over 1.8 million adolescent girls were out of school in 2009 (UNESCO, 2011).

The adult literacy rate in the country is also of concern. Statistics from 2009 indicate that 82% of Ethiopian women aged fifteen and over are illiterate, compared to 58% of men (UNESCO, 2011). Poverty is one of the main barriers to girls' and women's education. Socio-cultural factors such as social norms and traditional practices regarding the role and position of women in Ethiopian society, gender-based violence, early marriage, and teenage pregnancy affect girls' and women's' access to and completion of education. There are also various school-related factors affecting educational opportunities for girls. The lack of motivated and gender-sensitive teachers, girl-friendly school environments, targeted interventions to support girls, and quality education, as well as long distances to school, all negatively affect the chances of girls' access to and retention in secondary education.

Likewise, data from 2008 to 2012 provided by UNICEF also indicates a significant gender gap in primary and secondary education in Angola. Free primary education for all is an Angolan government policy, but unfortunately this has not translated into a reality that sees all children receiving education. According to the non-governmental organization Save the Children, about one third of the country's boys and girls do not attend school (Redvers, 2009). However, despite government efforts, the demand for education has not been met. It also seems that girls are the biggest victims because they are kept at home by their parents to run the household and look after siblings. The fact that girls are expected to help with household responsibilities is opening up a gulf in literacy rates between the two sexes. According to 2007 figures from the UNICEF, 84% of boys and only 63% of girls were literate. In addition, high teenage pregnancy rates perpetuate the problem, trapping many young women in a life of poverty. More than half of Angolan girls between the ages of fifteen to nineteen have at least one child (Redvers, 2009). First enrolment and the early grades are relatively equal for both boys and girls. However, by fourth grade, a lot more girls drop out, often because of family pressures to take on household responsibilities. Many girls leave school because they get pregnant. Usually, girls who drop out while still illiterate or barely literate have little opportunity of improving their economic situation and mostly end up as informal street traders.

In Uganda, girls are often denied the same educational opportunities as boys due to cultural attitudes and poverty. A major reason for girls' reduced educational opportunities is a result of how the role of women and girls in daily life is perceived by themselves and their communities. Uganda's fertility rate is 6.7, reaching over 7.5 in some rural areas (Daumerie and Madson, 2010). With the major role of women often being linked to childbearing and unpaid domestic duties, their education becomes a lower priority than that of boys. Without an education, girls miss out on fulfilling their social and economic potential. As girls' education continues to be valued less than boys', this is likely to reduce their access to education even further. The deep structural inequalities and disparities that keep girls out of school are hinged on a number of factors such as child labour (with more girls helping at home), and poverty, which usually causes early marriages. More males compared to females are enrolled in school among all age groups. Gender parity in primary school has almost been reached, although for every 100 girls aged three to five in the country, fewer than seven actually study in pre-primary. Like in pre-primary, secondary education is still a challenge as only twenty-two girls out of 100 aged thirteen to eighteen years are enrolled in secondary school, leaving a very big gap (Uganda Bureau of Statistics, 2012). The ninety-three out of 100 girls that are not attending pre-primary are an indication of little parental interest in early childhood development. The seventy-eight out of 100 girls that are not accessing secondary level education results in a number of challenges, including early marriages and hence low education levels of the mothers. According to the data, about four of every ten female leaders of the households in Uganda did not have formal education (Uganda Bureau of Statistics, 2012). This may have considerable effects on the welfare of the entire home.

Similarly in Burundi, despite the introduction of free primary education for all in 2005, there remains a large disparity between boys and girls as concerns education, particularly in secondary and higher education. Only 5% of eligible females are enrolled in secondary school (Freedom House, 2009b).

3.9 Discrimination

3.9.1 Nigeria and Ethiopia

Throughout Nigeria, women also experience discrimination in employment and are often relegated to inferior positions. Moreover, Nigerian women have very limited ownership rights. Civil laws entitle women to have access to land and a few States have enshrined equal inheritance rights into law, but certain customary laws stipulate that only men have the right to inherit and own land. Women in Purdah (Muslim communities in the northern areas) cannot leave their homes without permission from their husbands and must be accompanied by a man at all times when in public. Purdah also restricts women's freedom of dress, i.e. Muslim women must be veiled in public. Widows in these regions face the greatest degree of discrimination; they are confined to the home and must keep their heads shaven and wear mourning dress. More broadly, security officials have restricted freedom of movement by enforcing curfews in areas where terrorist activity or ethno-religious violence has taken place. Checkpoints and roadblocks are occasionally reported to have used excessive force or extorted money and goods from travellers (OECD, 2014d). In civil marriages, the mother and the father share parental authority and married couples jointly share legal responsibility for maintaining the family's financial expenses. Married and unmarried women can be the 'head of the household' in the same way as a man. However, at least two thirds of the Nigerian population are bound by customary and Islamic law that solely grants men the status of head of household and sole parental authority. Due to fear of ostracism, losing custody of children, or being unable to support themselves, many women may refrain from initiating divorce. Women and men have the same rights to vote and stand for elections in Nigeria; however, women comprise only a small percentage of elected officials in Nigeria.

Similarly in Ethiopia, women enjoy little independent decision making on most individual and family issues, including the option to choose whether to give birth in a health facility or seek medical assistance from trained providers (Alemu and Asnake, 2007). Regarding parental authority, the 2001 Family Code (Arts. 49 and 50) grants equal rights to parents. Both men and women may initiate divorce in Ethiopia. However, women who separate from their husbands are likely to lose their houses and property, and when a husband dies, other family members often claim the land over his widow. The 2005 DHS reported that 20% of widows reported being dispossessed of their land (OECD, 2014c). Women's ownership rights are limited in Ethiopia. Since 1997, reforms have improved access to land by stipulating that women have the right to lease land from the government, a right also granted in the Federal Constitution. Although Art. 35 of the Constitution grants women and men equal rights in matters of inheritance, traditional customs vary by region but usually pass land to sons on the ground that daughters eventually move into their husbands' homes. Thus, in practice, women's land rights are often ignored. Further, there are reports that in some instances widows are obliged to marry a male relative of the deceased spouse (OECD, 2014c). Freedom of movement is restricted in certain parts of Ethiopia on account of national security concerns. There do not appear to be any legal restrictions specifically on women's freedom of access to public spaces; however, some women may face restrictions on a day-to-day basis. Regarding political voice, there are no known quotas to encourage women's participation in politics in Ethiopia; women have the same rights as men to vote and run for election to political office. As of 2009, 13% of the top positions in both the executive and judicial branches were held by women; among higher-level positions below the ministers and judges, women held 26.6% of positions. That same year, Ethiopia ranked third in African countries in the number of women in parliament (OECD, 2014c).

3.9.2 *Angola*

In Angola, discriminatory practices towards women are common in private enterprises and, despite a non-discriminatory labour law, the public sector still remains inequitable in gender representation. The African Development Bank (2008) reports that women in Angola particularly struggle in accessing credit, often due to illiteracy or because they do not have assets that lenders require. There are no reported legal restrictions on access to public spaces for women in Angola, but the threat of sexual violence presents a significant barrier to women's freedom of movement. Further, Freedom House (2009) reports that women are often killed or injured by landmines as they search for food and firewood. Eight provinces (50% of the country) in 2009 contained areas that were heavily mined, restricting freedom of movement. At least 80,000 people have lost limbs to mines over the years (Freedom House, 2009a).

Both spouses may initiate divorce, as established by the Civil Code. No evidence of discrimination was found. With respect to inheritance rights, the Family Code provides for the inheritance rights of daughters. However, as a matter of practice under customary law, daughters may not inherit land or may inherit a smaller amount than sons. The inheritance rights of widows and divorced women are particularly precarious. Although divorced women or widows may inherit land, this is commonly only in trust for their children. A study conducted by the Rural Development Institute in 2008 found that only 23% of widows use the land left by their deceased husbands and further, that many women lack knowledge of their land and inheritance rights. The 1992 Land Act (updated in 2004) provides women and men with equal rights. However, evidence suggests that land distribution follows customary practices that tend to disadvantage women. Women's rights to land do differ by region and between ethnic groups according to their social structures (patrilineal or matrilineal) and the farming system introduced during colonial times.

As presented earlier, women enjoy legal protections and occupy cabinet positions and national assembly seats, but *de facto* discrimination and violence against women remain common, particularly in rural areas. With respect to women's political voice, 30% quotas in the single lower house have been introduced in 2010. There were no quotas in 2009.

3.9.3 *Uganda and Burundi*

In Uganda, only 36.41% of widows inherited the majority of assets after their spouse's death in 2006, as over 75% of land in Uganda is held under the customary law system (OECD, 2014e). In some areas, if a man dies, his brother can 'inherit' the man's widow. Widows that reject remarriages within the clan can be punished by confiscation of land, children, shelter, and household property (The Coalition Against Gender Violence and UNFPA, 2004). Discriminatory customary practices persist in regard to women's land rights, despite the government's recent adoption of a Land Act (2004) designed to improve women's access to land and grant them the right to manage their property. According to the International Monetary Fund, although approximately 70% of women are employed in agricultural activities, only 20% own land (OECD, 2014e).

Similarly in Burundi, inheritance is largely governed by customary laws that discriminate against women. Under customary law, rural women cannot inherit from their fathers or from their husbands and often their brothers will not welcome them back into their family homes, leaving widows landless and homeless. Women and men have the right to initiate divorce under the civil code. Women have limited opportunities for advancement in the economic and political sphere, especially in rural areas.

3.10 Law enforcement

3.10.1 Nigeria and Ethiopia

The 1999 Constitution of Nigeria prohibits discrimination on the basis of sex, but customary and religious laws continue to restrict women's rights. Although an Abolition of All Forms of Discrimination against Women in Nigeria and other related matters bill was considered in the mid-2000s, the national assembly did not pass this bill nor a related national bill prohibiting violence against women. Nigeria ratified the CEDAW in 1985 and the Optional Protocol in 2004. The country ratified the African Charter on Human and People's Rights (ACHPR) in 1983 and the Protocol to the African Charter on Human and People's Rights on the Rights of Women in Africa (PACHPRRWA) in 2005. There are no legislated quotas at either the national or sub-national level to promote women's political participation. However, there is an active and vocal women's movement in Nigeria, which provides practical support to women (i.e. shelters for victims of domestic violence and credit schemes), as well as advocating women's rights at the national level in regard to reproductive health, marriage, employment, and political participation and pushing for changes to discriminatory legislation.

From 1991 to 1995 Ethiopia had a Women's Affairs Department in the office of the prime minister. In 1995, this was changed to a separate ministry: the Ministry of Women's Affairs. However, the ministry suffered from insufficient decision-making power and inadequate human and financial resources in order to effectively promote the advancement of women and gender equality (ACGSD, 2010). The government also established a National Committee on Traditional Practices of Ethiopia (NCTPE) to conduct research and make recommendations about such practices. Civil society organizations such as the Network of Ethiopian Women Association (NEWA) and the Ethiopian Women Lawyers Association (EWLA) play a significant role in furthering women's rights and making the government accountable. The Constitution ensures gender equality and incorporates the major UN conventions on human rights and elimination of all forms of discrimination against women. The Constitution acknowledges the duty of the State to protect women from the influence of harmful customary practices, stating that all laws, stereotypes, ideas, and customs that oppress women or otherwise adversely affect their physical and mental well-being are prohibited (ACGSD, 2010). Ethiopia also ratified the CEDAW in 1981, the ACHPR in 1998, and the PACHPRRWA in 2004.

The Criminal Code was revised in 2004 to punish the crimes of abduction, rape, and other forms of sexual assault. Rape sentences have increased to twenty-five years imprisonment. However, most of the cases are settled out of court and, in some circumstances, if the perpetrator agrees to marry the victim, amnesty is granted. Moreover, this does not include spousal rape. The revised Criminal Code also outlaws violence against a spouse or partner.

FGM is forbidden. The revised Criminal Code criminalized FGM with no less than three months in prison or a fine for those that practise it. Infibulation is also punishable by imprisonment of five to ten years. However, no criminal prosecutions have been instituted so far (ACGSD, 2010). The government has been involved with NGOs in anti-FGM education. The Ministry of Education includes information discouraging FGM in educational materials. The government has also been supportive of the Committee on Traditional Practices of Ethiopia.

The National Action Plan for Gender Equality 2006–2010 sets a number of priorities, among which is the elimination of traditional practices harmful to women's health (ACGSD, 2010). The Ministry of Justice has established a special unit for the investigation and prosecution of violence with due emphasis on sexual violence. Other offences created and criminalized by the revised Criminal Code include endangering the lives of children and pregnant women through harmful traditional practices; causing bodily injury to children and pregnant women through harmful traditional practices; and causing bodily injuries through other harmful traditional practices. The amended Code also punishes trafficking in women and children and early marriages, and regulates widow inheritance (ACGSD, 2010). In 2000 the Family Code raised the legal age of marriage from fifteen to eighteen. Early marriage is nevertheless common, particularly in rural areas, and affects children far younger than the legal age. This still happens because early marriage has historically been viewed as ensuring girls' social integration and thereby their protection, as well as their moral and social development (OECD, 2014c).

3.10.2 Angola

In 2007, the government of Angola helped to draw up the joint Ministerial Conference of the Economic Community of West African States (ECOWAS) and Economic Community of Central African States' (ECCAS) plan of action to control trafficking in persons, especially women and children. The government of Angola – with technical and financial support from UNFPA, the UN Development Program (UNDP), and the UN Development Fund for Women (UNIFEM) – implemented a four-year program (2005–2008) to build the capacity of the Ministry of Family and the Promotion of Women, as well as its NGO partners such as the Organization of Angolan Women (OMA) and Rede Mulher, an Angolan non-governmental organization focussing on women's issues.

Specifically, it addresses the need to build and strengthen national capacity for advocating and mainstreaming gender and human rights. The State Secretariat for the Promotion and Development of Women, created in 1991, was upgraded to the Ministry of Family and the Promotion of Women in 1997. In addition to its responsibility for the formulation and implementation of a national policy on the rights of women, focal points exist in other ministries to mainstream gender in government policies, programs, and projects. One of these programs seeks to eradicate gender-based poverty through the provision of counselling, legal aid, microcredit, and other interventions for rural women. In 2001, the Angolan government started family counseling centres and partnered with the Angolan Bar Association to give free legal assistance to abused women. The Ministry of Family and the Promotion of Women has also undertaken information campaigns on domestic abuse in the framework of Human Rights Day. The campaigns include full-page articles and announcements on public radio.

The Constitution of Angola formally acknowledges women's rights to equality and prohibits discrimination on the basis of sex. Angola has also ratified the ACHPR in 1990, the CEDAW in 1986, the Optional Protocol to CEDAW in 2007, the PACHPRRWA in 2007, the Southern African Declaration on Gender and Development in 1997 (SADCDGD), and the Addendum to SADCDGD in 1998. In 2008, the government approved a National Action Plan against domestic violence. The plan includes strategies to publicize the CEDAW and family law among citizens to create awareness of women's rights.

Rape, battery, and assault are criminalized under the Penal Code and punishable by up to eight years imprisonment, though the underreporting of violence and an ineffectual judicial system prevent prosecution in most cases. Sexual harassment is not illegal, though it can be prosecuted in certain cases under assault and battery statutes in the Penal Code. The Angola Civil Code sets the legal age of marriage in Angola at sixteen years for both sexes; however, the law allows for girls to be married at a younger age in special circumstances. The Family Code establishes equality between men and women within the family; both spouses have the same rights and are subject to the same duties. These principles extend to matters of parental authority. The Family Code prescribes that both parents have equal responsibility to support their children, and if the children remain with the mother after a divorce, the father must pay for the maintenance of the children. However, the Rural Development Institute found in a study on women's land rights in Angola that although property tends to be divided equally post-divorce without court interference, in cases where it is not or when women are abandoned by their husbands, there was little evidence that women pursued their rights to property through legal channels (OECD, 2014a).

3.10.3 Uganda

In November 2009, the Ugandan parliament passed the country's first bill criminalizing domestic violence, the Domestic Violence Act, which was signed into law in 2010. The bill provides a thorough definition of domestic violence that includes physical, sexual, emotional, verbal, psychological, and economic violence as well as harassment. In addition, the bill provides protection orders for abused women, which had not previously existed in Ugandan law (OECD, 2014e). Rape is a criminal offence in Uganda under Chapter 14 of the Penal Code, which also prescribes the death penalty for those convicted of rape. Spousal rape is not recognized as a criminal offence, but the Marriage and Divorce Act and the Draft Sexual Offences Bill of 2004 (both pending in 2009) recognized spousal rape as a crime and mandated imprisonment, fines, and compensation to the victim as punishment if the partner's refusal to have sex is on the basis of poor health, surgery that affects the capacity to engage in sexual intercourse, childbirth, or reasonable fear that engaging in sexual intercourse is likely to cause physical or psychological injury or harm (OECD, 2014e). The amount of compensation shall take into account factors such as medical and other expenses incurred by the victim (ACGSD, 2010).

In order to scale up efforts to curb gender-based violence in the country, a Gender Based Violence Reference Group was established in 2006. This is a technical advisory group that coordinates and provides oversight to the implementation of GBV interventions. The reference group consists of representation from justice, law and order, and health and social development sectors as well as civil society organizations and development partners. The reference group has had a number of achievements such as the establishment of training standards and the inclusion of a domestic violence module in the Uganda DHS (2005) and the National Household Surveys, advocating and coordinating legal, health, and psychosocial support responses to gender-based violence. The group has also played an important role in advocating for enactment of gender-related bills such as the Marriage and Divorce Bill, Domestic Violence Bill, Trafficking in Persons Bill, and the Bill on Prohibition of Female Genital Mutilation (ACGSD, 2010). Uganda ratified the CEDAW in 1985, the ACHPR in 1986, and the PACHPRRWA in 2003. It also signed the Palermo Protocol in 2000. Regarding quotas, the government has taken special legislative measures to increase women's political participation. These include a constitutional article (78(1)) that states that Parliament should have one female representative for each of the 112 districts in Uganda, and a 2006 electoral law that requires that these representatives be selected from an all-female ballot. Women must make up one third of local councils, which share jurisdiction with magistrate courts on decisions pertaining to local customs (Constitution of Uganda, 1995 – Art. 180 (2)).

The 1995 Constitution of Uganda provides that 'women shall be accorded full and equal dignity of the person with men' (Article 33(1)) and further provides that 'the State shall provide the facilities and opportunities necessary to enhance the welfare of the women to enable them to realize their full potential' (Article 33(2)). Moreover, the Constitution provides that 'laws, cultures, customs or tradition against the dignity, welfare or interest of women are prohibited by the Constitution' (Article 33(6)) (OECD, 2014e). However, as noted above, there are many cultural practices still in place that conflict with the Constitution. Nevertheless, although the Constitution enshrines the principle of equality between women and men, discrimination against women remains pronounced, particularly in rural areas.

Regarding parental authority there are no known laws which stipulate that men must be heads of the households. However, marital practices are governed by different customary legal systems, which determine family law. Many of these discriminate against women. Under the Marriage Act, widows have the right to inherit 15% of a deceased husband's property. However, customary laws dictate that women do not have the right to inherit.

Finally, the International Criminal Court has also issued indictments against the LRA commanders who were indicted for crimes against humanity including sexual enslavement, rape, mutilation, and abduction of girls (Amnesty International, 2007). In fact, as presented previously, rape and other forms of sexual violence have been ongoing features of the conflict in northern Uganda over the past two decades; the LRA has made consistent use of rape, sexual mutilation, and the abduction of male and female children for sexual slavery. There have been also cases of rape being used by security forces as a means of torture and intimidation (OECD, 2014e). Sexual harassment is a criminal offence with penalties of up to fourteen years imprisonment, but the law is not effectively enforced. Nevertheless, sexual harassment is reportedly widespread in schools, hospitals, and workplaces in Uganda (OECD, 2014e).

3.10.4 Burundi

In Burundi, Article 12 of the Constitutional Act of Transition of 1998 states that respect for the rights and duties proclaimed and guaranteed by the Universal Declaration of Human Rights, the international rights covenants, the African Charter on Human and Peoples Rights, and the Charter of National Unity are guaranteed by the Constitutional Act. Article 17 states that all persons are equal before the law in dignity and in rights and duties without discrimination as to sex, origin, race, religion, or beliefs. All are equal before the law and are entitled without discrimination to equal protection before the law (ACGSD, 2010). Burundi ratified the ACHPR in 1989 and the CEDAW in 1992 and signed the Palermo Protocol in 2000, the Optional Protocol to CEDAW in 2001, and the PACHPRRWA in 2003. The Code of Persons and the Family contains a number of measures eliminating discrimination against women, including the abolition of polygamy and unilateral repudiation of marriage, and introducing legal divorce and regulation of the age of marriage. The Code of Persons and the Family was modified in 1993 to amend discriminatory provisions. Despite having a formal legal system that ensures gender equality, important aspects of family life (such as matrimonial arrangements, successions, legacies, and gifts related to marriage) are still governed by customary laws.

Under Art. 88 of the Code of Persons and the Family, the legal age of marriage in Burundi is eighteen years for women and twenty-one for men. However, exceptions to these provisions based on serious causes (not specified) can be approved by the provincial governor. Forced marriages are prohibited under Art. 29 of the Constitution. Art. 145 of the Code of Persons and the Family, however, protects marriages contracted between underaged individuals if the underaged wife is pregnant or has already given birth (OECD, 2014b). According to the 1993 amendments, men and women share parental authority and have equal rights and responsibilities in regard to guardianship, trusteeship, and adoption of children. However, Art. 22 of the Code of Persons and the Family provides that the male is the head of the household, thereby codifying the unequal position of the woman in the family. The woman can become the head of the household only in the man's absence or if he faces a legal restriction.

The Criminal Code and Criminal Procedure Code do not effectively protect women from violence (OECD, 2014b), though rape and gender-based violence are criminalized under Art. 559 of Burundi's revised Criminal Code. A 2009 revision the Penal Code (Law No. 1/05) defines rape and provides for its punishment (Art. 554 and 558), including life imprisonment as one of the available penalties. It also criminalizes marital rape, although the punishment is only eight days imprisonment and a fine (OECD, 2014b). Reforms to the Penal Code specifically criminalize domestic violence, with penalties of three to five years. The Penal Code defines the crime of adultery in terms more favourable to men than to women.

The principle of gender equality and non-discrimination on the grounds of sex is enshrined in the 2005 Constitution, and according to the Personal Status and Family Code (Art. 159), sons and daughters have equal inheritance rights, though surviving female spouses do not. The Nationality Code of Burundi does not grant women equal rights with men regarding the nationality of their children.

Art. 164 of the 2004 Constitution reserves 30% of national assembly, senate, and ministerial positions for women. Art. 38.3 of the Electoral Code establishes that the electoral candidate lists must take into account gender balance, with one woman for every four candidates. However, the Global Network for Women Peacebuilders noted that legislated quotas are not strictly observed in practice (OECD, 2014b).

4 Analysis and results

4.1 Limitations of the study

The major limitation of the research is the limited temporal/space domain. Given this limitation, it is not possible to generalize the results. It is not possible to get to a general conclusion on the correlation between gender equality and genocide, but only to observe and describe this correlation in five sub-Saharan countries. Moreover, the analysed data do not necessarily show a cause-effect relationship, but just the variation of one variable according to the variation of another variable. However, because I am convinced that gender indicators might be one of the missing elements in the existing genocide prevention models, I decided to focus my research on testing the correlation between gender equality and genocide anyway, even though I am aware that generalizability of results is not possible and that this work presents just a 'first step' into a new research field. Howbeit, present limitations might be overcome through future research. The divulgation of primary data on social, economic, and health gender equality and the data on female participation both in the public and private process might help to overcome the space/temporal limitation of the results. Indeed, with available primary data, it might be possible to enlarge the spectrum of analysed countries by comparing different regions of the world, conducting a cross-longitudinal study, and finally, generalizing the results concluding whether it is possible or not to state that there is a causal relationship between gender equality and genocide.

4.2 Year of the research

I chose 2009 as the year of my analysis to measure the influence of gender equality in the five case studies, because both data on gender equality and Country Risks of Genocide and Politicide Index Score of genocide were available for 2009. I also considered 2009 to be a good option because the genocide in Nigeria started in 2010, and 2009 allowed me to measure gender equality the year before the eruption of violence, knowing that gender-based violence is usually reported to increase during genocide. In this way, the results would not have been vitiated by the increase of sexual and gender-based violence during the genocide. I chose 2009 even though the genocide in Ethiopia started between 2005 and 2006 because Harff and Gurr's Risk Index Score data are available only from 2007 on. Moreover, gender equality in all five case studies in the period from 2006 to 2009 (there is no available Global Gender Gap Report before 2006) did not register gross changes in ranking, thus I could use for my research data posterior to 2005 also for Ethiopia, without risking that they would have been vitiated by an increase of sexual and gender-based violence during the genocide. I also chose 2009 because the data elaborated by Barbara Harff were available since 2007 but not those of Genocide Watch (which released its first report in 2008 and which I used to check the accuracy of Harff and Gurr's Risk Index Score). However, I reviewed the data of 2008 and 2009 and I still preferred to choose 2009 because, in my opinion, data of 2009 are the most accurate. Moreover, it is only for 2009 that data for every case study is available.

4.3 Data used for the research

4.3.1 Social Institutions and Gender Index (SIGI)

SIGI released its first dataset in 2009. It covers non-OECD and non-EU countries that have a population of over one million. The focus is on developing countries undergoing rapid political, economic, and social development. The surveyed countries number 160, allowing cross-country, regional, and sub-regional analyses. It encompasses thirty-three indicators on gender discrimination in social institutions in five categories (i.e. discriminatory family code, restricted physical integrity, son bias, restricted access to resources and assets, and restricted civil liberties). The *Discriminatory Family Code* is composed of the legal age of marriage (whether women and men have the same legal minimum age of marriage), early marriage (i.e. percentage of women married between fifteen to nineteen years of age), parental authority in marriage (whether women and men have the same right to be the legal guardian of a child during marriage), parental authority in divorce (whether women and men have the same right to be the legal guardian of and have custody rights over a child after divorce), inheritance rights of widows (whether widows and widowers have equal inheritance rights), and inheritance rights of daughters (whether daughters and sons have equal inheritance rights). The *Restricted Physical Integrity Code* considers the laws on domestic violence (whether the legal framework offers women legal protection from domestic violence), laws on rape (whether the legal framework offers women legal protection from rape), laws on sexual harassment (whether the legal framework offers women legal protection from sexual harassment), attitudes toward violence (i.e. percentage of women who agree that a husband/partner is justified in beating his wife/partner under certain circumstances), prevalence of violence in the lifetime (i.e. percentage of women who have experienced physical and/or sexual violence from an intimate partner at some time in their lives), female genital mutilation prevalence (i.e. percentage of women who have undergone any type of female genital mutilation), reproductive autonomy/unmet need for family planning (percentage of married women aged fifteen to forty-nine with an unmet need for family planning, i.e. women who do not want any more children for the next two years and who are not using contraception).

The *Son Bias Code* is composed of the shortfall in the number of women in sex ratios for ages 0–4, 5–9, 10–14, 15–64, and 65+ (relative to the expected number if there were no sex-selective abortions, no female infanticide, or similar levels of healthcare and nutrition) and fertility preferences (i.e. share of males as the last child of women currently not desiring additional children or sterilized). The *Restricted Resources and Assets Code* considers secure access to land (whether women and men have equal and secure access to land use, control, and ownership), secure access to non-land assets (whether women and men have equal and secure access to non-land assets use, control, and ownership), and access to financial services (whether women and men have equal access to financial services).

The *Restricted Civil Liberties Code* is composed of access to public space (whether women face restrictions on their freedom of movement and access to public space, such as restricted ability to choose their places of residence, visit their families and friends, or to apply for a passport), political voice quotas (whether there are legal quotas to promote women's political participation at national and sub-national levels), and political representation (i.e. share of women in national parliaments). The SIGI Index includes variables that are often overlooked in other composite gender equality indices. Discriminatory social institutions are defined as the formal and informal laws, attitudes, and practices that restrict women's' and girls' access to rights, justice, and empowerment opportunities (OECD Development Centre [OECD DEV], 2009). These are captured in a multi-faceted approach by SIGI's variables that combine qualitative and quantitative data, taking into account both the *de jure* and *de facto* discrimination of social institutions, through information on laws, attitudes, and practices. The variables span all stages of a woman's life in order to show how discriminatory social institutions can interlock and bind them into cycles of disempowerment and poverty. The level of discrimination against women is captured through a multi-dimensional assessment that takes into account the legislative framework, the *de facto* situation (i.e. customary laws and practices, implementation of laws, etc.), and practices through prevalence data and attitudinal data. In addition to economic and social indicators (i.e. employment or education) the SIGI focuses on social norms, offering an analytical lens to explain persistent gaps in these outcomes between women and men. The SIGI combines both qualitative and quantitative research for each country noted, giving priority to national data sources where available. The technical construction of the SIGI verifies statistical association and conceptual relevance and fits an axiomatic requirement for such measures of inequalities (OECD DEV., 2009).

4.3.2 Global Gender Gap Report

The Global Gender Gap Index, derived from analysis reported in the Global Gender Gap Report (introduced in 2006 by the World Economic Forum), is a framework for capturing the magnitude and scope of gender-based disparities and tracking their progress. The Index benchmarks national gender gaps on health-based, educational, economic, and political criteria, and provides country rankings that allow for effective comparisons over time and across regions and income groups. There are three basic concepts underlying the Global Gender Gap Index. First, it focuses on measuring gaps rather than levels. Second, it captures gaps in outcome variables rather than gaps in means or input variables. Third, it ranks countries according to gender equality rather than women's empowerment (World Economic Forum, 2006). The Index is designed to measure gender-based gaps in access to resources and opportunities in individual countries rather than the actual levels of the available resources and opportunities in those countries. It evaluates countries based on outcome variables rather than input measures. The aim is to provide a picture of where men and women stand with regard to some fundamental outcome variables related to basic rights such as health, education, economic participation, and political empowerment. The third distinguishing feature of the Global Gender Gap Index is that it ranks countries according to their proximity to gender equality rather than to women's empowerment. The Global Gender Gap Index examines the gap between men and women in four fundamental categories: health and survival, educational attainment, political empowerment, and economic participation and opportunity. Health and survival are measured by using the gap between women's and men's healthy life expectancy, calculated by the World Health Organization. This measure provides an estimate of the number of years that women and men can expect to live in good health by taking into account the years lost to violence, disease, malnutrition, or other relevant factors. The second variable included in this sub-index is the sex ratio at birth. This variable aims specifically to capture the phenomenon of 'missing women' prevalent in many countries with strong son preference.

In the educational attainment category, the gap between women's and men's current access to education is captured through ratios of women to men in primary, secondary, and tertiary level education. A longer-term view of the country's ability to educate women and men in equal numbers is captured through the ratio of the female literacy rate to the male literacy rate. The economic participation and opportunity are captured through the participation gap, the remuneration gap, and the advancement gap. The participation gap is captured through the difference in labour force participation rates. The remuneration gap is captured through the ratio of estimated female-to-male earned income and through wage equality for similar work (calculated through the World Economic Forum's Executive Opinion Survey). Finally, the gap between the advancement of women and men is captured through the ratio of women to men among legislators, senior officials and managers, and the ratio of women to men among technical and professional workers.

The category of political empowerment includes mainly measures of the gap between men and women in political decision making at the highest levels. This concept is captured through the ratio of women to men in minister-level positions and the ratio of women to men in parliamentary positions. In addition, the report includes the ratio of women to men in terms of years in executive office (prime minister or president) in the last fifty years.

4.3.3 Genocide Watch

Genocide Watch exists to predict, prevent, stop, and punish genocide and other forms of mass atrocities. It seeks to raise awareness and influence public policy concerning potential and actual genocide (Genocide Watch, 1999). Genocide Watch monitors high-risk areas and declares 'Genocide Watches' (when early warning signs indicate the danger of mass killing or genocide), 'Genocide Warnings' (when politicide or genocide is imminent, often indicated by genocidal massacres), and 'Genocide Emergencies' (when genocide is actually underway). It also recommends options for governments, international organizations, and non-governmental organizations to prevent genocide. It uses predictive models such as Gregory Stanton's 'Ten Stages of Genocide' to analyse high-risk situations for the purpose of education, policy analysis, and advocacy. According to this model, genocide is a process that develops in ten stages that are predictable but not inexorable. At each stage, preventive measures can stop it. The process is not linear and stages may occur simultaneously. Logically, earlier stages must precede later stages. However, all stages continue to operate throughout the process. The stages of genocide are classification, symbolization, discrimination, dehumanization, organization, polarization, preparation, persecution, extermination, and denial.

All cultures have categories to distinguish people into 'us and them' by ethnicity, race, nationality, or religion (e.g. German and Jew, Hutu and Tutsi). Bipolar societies that lack mixed categories are the most likely to have genocide. *Classification* and *symbolization* are universally human and do not necessarily result in genocide unless they lead to dehumanization. When combined with hatred, symbols may be forced upon unwilling members of the pariah group (e.g. the yellow star for Jews under Nazi rule, the blue scarf for people from the Eastern Zone in Khmer Rouge Cambodia) (Genocide Watch, 2013).

Discrimination starts when a dominant group uses law, custom, and political power to deny the rights of another group. The powerless group may not be accorded full civil rights, voting rights, or even citizenship. The dominant group is driven by an exclusionary ideology that would deprive the less powerful group of its rights. The ideology advocates monopolization or expansion of power by the dominant group and it legitimizes the victimization of weaker groups. *Dehumanization* may follow. One group denies the humanity of the other group. Members of the dehumanized group are equated with animals, insects, or diseases. Dehumanization overcomes the normal human revulsion against murder. At this stage, hate propaganda is used to vilify the victim group. The majority group is taught to regard the other group as less than human, and even alien to their society. The powerless group can become so depersonalized that its members are actually given numbers rather than names (e.g. Jews in the death camps) (Genocide Watch, 2013). They are equated with immorality, impurity, and dirt. Moreover, genocide is always 'organized' (sometimes by the State), often using militias to provide deniability of State responsibility (e.g. the Janjaweed in Darfur). Other times *organization* is informal (e.g. Hindu mobs led by local RSS militants) or decentralized (e.g. terrorist groups) (Genocide Watch, 2013). Special army units or militias are often trained and armed. Plans are made for genocidal killings and acts of genocide are disguised as counterinsurgency if there is an ongoing armed conflict or civil war.

During the stage of *polarization*, extremists drive the groups apart. Hate groups broadcast polarizing propaganda. Laws may forbid intermarriage or social interaction. Extremist terrorism targets moderates, intimidating and silencing the centre. Moderates from the perpetrators' own group are most able to stop genocide, so are the first to be arrested and killed. Leaders in targeted groups are the next to be arrested and murdered. The dominant group passes emergency laws or decrees that grants them total power over the targeted group. The laws erode fundamental civil rights and liberties.

Targeted groups are disarmed to make them incapable of self-defence and to ensure that the dominant group has total control.

During stage seven (*preparation*), national or perpetrator group leaders plan the 'final solution'. They often use euphemisms to hide their intentions, such as referring to their goals as 'counter-terrorism' or 'purification', disguising genocide as 'self-defence'. They build armies, buy weapons, and train their troops and militias and they indoctrinate the population with fear of the victim group. There is a sudden increase in inflammatory rhetoric and hate propaganda with the objective of creating fear of the other group.

During *persecution*, death lists are drawn up. Victims are identified and separated out because of their ethnic or religious identity. Their property is often expropriated. Sometimes they are even segregated into ghettoes, deported into concentration camps, or confined to a famine-struck region and starved. They are deliberately deprived of resources such as water or food in order to slowly destroy them. Programs are implemented to prevent procreation through forced sterilization or abortions. Children are forcibly taken from their parents. The victim group's basic human rights become systematically abused through forced displacement, torture, and extrajudicial killings. *Extermination* begins, and quickly becomes the mass killing legally called 'genocide'. It is 'extermination' to the killers because they do not believe their victims to be fully human. Sometimes the genocide results in revenge killings by groups against each other, creating the cycle of bilateral genocide (as in the case of Burundi). Acts of genocide demonstrate how dehumanized the victims have become. Already dead bodies are dismembered, men of fighting age are murdered, and rape is used as a tool of war to genetically alter and eradicate the other group. Destruction of cultural and religious property is employed to annihilate the group's existence from history. In total genocides all the members of the targeted group are exterminated.

The final stage is usually *denial*. It is among the surest indicators of further genocidal massacres. The perpetrators of genocide try to cover up the evidence by digging up mass graves, burning the bodies, and intimidating witnesses. They deny that they committed any crimes, and often blame what happened on the victims. They block investigations of the crimes and continue to govern until driven from power by force, when they flee into exile. This model demonstrates that there is logic to the genocidal process, though it may not proceed in a linear order.

4.3.4 Country Risks of Genocide and Politicide Index Score

This score is derived from analyses reported in Barbara Harff (2003). That study used data from all countries with internal wars and regime failures from 1955 to 2001. The presence of six risk factors, in various combinations, contributed to the subsequent occurrence of genocide or politicide. The variables used in the Country Risks of Genocide and Politicide Index Score are:

- Instability scores: countries with instability ledger scores greater than 20 are given weights of +3; if ledger scores are 10 to 19.9, the weight is 2; if 2 to 5.9, the weight is −1; if less than 2 (i.e. highly stable countries), the weight is −2.

- State-led discrimination: State policies and practices deliberately restrict the economic and/or political rights of specific minority groups. Derived from the analyses by the Minorities at Risk project (University of Maryland).

- Genocides and politicides since 1955: this is an important variable in defining the causes that led to genocide because perpetrators are often repeat offenders. This is because elites and security forces may become habituated to mass killings as a strategic response to challenges to State security and also, because targeted groups are rarely destroyed in their entirety.

- Ethnically polarized elite: this variable flags countries in which access to the political elite is intensely contested along ethnic, tribal, or other communal lines.

- Exclusionary ideology: the political elite holds a belief system that identifies some purpose or principle that justifies efforts to restrict, persecute, or eliminate specific political, class, ethnic, or religious groups.

- Current regime type: full autocracies (weighted 3.5 in risk analysis) have a score of −6 or lower on the polity scale, which ranges from −10 for full autocracies to +10 for full democracies. Full autocracies have been most likely to perpetrate genocides and politicides; partial autocracies (scores of −5 to 1, weighted 2) are somewhat less at risk. Partial democracies (weighted −2) have scores of +2 to +6; full democracies (weighted −3.5) have scores of +7 to +10. Countries with no effective regime or incoherent regimes (polity codes of −1, 0, +1, and −77) are given weights of 0.

- Trade openness (imports + exports as % of GNP, latest data available): signifies the extent of international engagement in a country. This indicator serves as a highly sensitive indicator of State and elite willingness to maintain the rules of law and fair practices in the economic sphere. Risks have been highest in countries with the lowest openness scores, 45 or less (weight of +2.5). Medium scores are 46–70 (weight of +1); high scores are 71–100 (weight of −1). The most highly interdependent countries, scores greater than 100, are given a weight of –2.5. An empirically and theoretically based risk score is derived for each country.

Major instances of instability, either internal war or abrupt regime changes, preceded most historical episodes of genocide and politicide. Therefore scholars added the likelihood of future instability in a country as an additional risk factor (Harff and Gurr, 2009). The risk factors are weighted according to their relative importance. Some risk scores are negative and thus are used to offset positive risk factors. For example, a partial or full democratic regime is substantially less likely to carry out genocide even if the country has other, positive risk factors. A high level of economic interdependence and a low risk of future instability have similar inhibiting effects. In addition, if a country has no State-led discrimination or no exclusionary ideology, those variables' weights are subtracted from the risk score. These factors are within the control of elites and governments and their absence implies positive State action to contain genocide-inducing factors. Finally, Harff and Gurr did not assign minus scores to countries that did not have past genocides because their histories cannot be changed, in contrast to active discrimination or exclusionary ideologies, both of which can be changed by government policy. As to elite polarization, no minus weights are assigned because the condition can rarely be actively altered in the short or medium run.

4.4 Standard deviation for gender equality and genocide, covariation, and Bravais-Pearson correlation coefficient

In statistics, the standard deviation (SD, also represented by the Greek letter sigma σ or the Latin letter s) is a measure that is used to quantify the amount of variation or dispersion of a set of data values. A low SD indicates that the data points tend to be close to the mean (also called the expected value) of the set, while a high SD indicates that the data points are spread out over a wider range of values.

The formula to calculate the standard deviation is:

$$\sigma = \frac{1}{N} \sum_{i=1}^{N} (x_1 - \mu)^2$$

N = number of variables
x_1 = country
μ = average of the considered variable

Covariance provides a measure of the strength of the correlation between two or more sets of random variates.
The formula to calculate covariance is:

$$cov(X,Y) = \sum_{i=1}^{N} \frac{(x_i - \bar{x})(y_i - \bar{y})}{N}$$

x_i = gender equality
$\bar{x}$ = average of gender equality
y_i = genocide
$\bar{y}$ = average of genocide
N = number of case studies

The correlation coefficient of Bravais-Pearson is a measure of the linear correlation between two variables x and y, giving a value between +1 and −1 inclusive, where 1 is total positive correlation, 0 is no correlation, and −1 is total negative correlation. It is widely used in the sciences as a measure of the degree of linear dependence between two variables. The + indicates a positive linear relationship, while the − indicates a negative linear relationship. A positive linear relationship is a form of linear relationship in which increases in the values of the first variable are accompanied by increases in the values of the second variable. Conversely, a negative correlation is a relationship between two variables in which one variable increases as the other decreases.
The formula to calculate the correlation coefficient of Bravais-Pearson is:

$$\rho = \frac{COVxy}{(Sx\,Sy)}$$

$COVxy$ = covariation between x and y
Sx = standard deviation of x
Sy = standard deviation of y
If $0 < \rho xy < 0.3$ the correlation is weak;
if $0.3 < \rho xy < 0.7$ the correlation is moderate;
if $\rho xy > 0.7$ the correlation is strong.

4.5 Results

As outlined previously, among the analysed case studies, only Ethiopia and Nigeria experienced genocide in 2006 and 2010, respectively.
According to Genocide Watch, in 2009 the genocide in Ethiopia was already underway, while in Nigeria, genocidal violence erupted in 2010.

Table 4.1 Country Risks of Genocide and Politicide Index Score (2009)

Countries and 2009 Risk Index Score	Problems and Conflict Issues	Risks of Future Instability weights +3 to −3	Targets of State-led Discrimination weights +2 to −2	Geno/Politicides since 1955 weights +3.5 to 0	Ethnically Polarized Elite weights +2.5 to 0	Exclusionary Ideology weights +2.5 to −2.5	Current Regime Type weights +3.5 to −3.5	Trade Openness weights +2.5 to −2.5
Angola 5.5	Ethnic separatism	Very high +3	Cabindans +2	Yes: 1975–2001 +3.5	No 0	No −2.5	Partial autocracy +2	Very high −2.5
Ethiopia 5.5	Separatism; ethnic/ religious cleavages	Very high +3	None −2	Yes: 1976–79 +3.5	Yes: Tigreans dominate +2.5	No −2.5	Mixed regime 0	Medium low +1
Burundi 3.5	Ethnic	Very high +3	None −2	Yes: 1965–73 1993, 1998 +3.5	Yes: Tutsis dominate +2.5	No −2.5	Partial democracy −2	Medium low +1
Uganda 3.5	Ethnic/regional, autonomist	High +2	None −2	Yes: 1980–83, 1985–86 +3.5	No 0	No −2.5	Mixed regime 0	Very low +2.5
Nigeria 3	Autonomy; north-south and religious cleavages	Very high + 3	Ogani, Ejaw +2	Yes: 1967–69 +3.5	No 0	No −2.5	Partial democracy −2	High −1

Table 4.1 is the Country Risks of Genocide and Politicide Index Score (2009), elaborated by Barbara Harff and Tedd Gurr.

According to this Risk Index Score, calculated by measuring all the variables that are usually considered to be those influencing the eruption of genocide, all the considered countries (with the exception of Uganda) were at very high risk of future instability. However, Ethiopia (where the genocide was already underway in 2009) got the same score of Angola where, according to Genocide Watch, the level of violence did not turn in genocidal violence, even after 2009. Moreover, Nigeria (the only country that experienced genocide after 2009) got the lowest score among the five case studies. Thus, even if considered one of the world's most reliable indexes for the prevision of genocide, according to the present analysis, there is something missing in the Risk Index Score elaborated by Harff and Gurr. My hypothesis is that one of these missing elements is gender equality. For this reason, to the usual considered variables I added an analysis on gender equality in the case studies to measure the weight that gender equality had on the eruption of genocidal violence, using the data elaborated by the Global Gender Gap Report of the World Economic Forum. Table 4.2 gives the resulting data about gender equality in the case studies, according to the Global Gender Gap Report (2009).

As outlined in Table 4.3, the two countries that experienced genocide are also the ones with lower gender equality scores.

Table 4.2 Global Gender Gap Report data (2009)

Country	Score
Burundi*	0.710
Uganda	0.707
Angola	0.635
Nigeria	0.628
Ethiopia	0.595

0.00 = inequality, 1.00 = equality
*Data elaborated using the scores from 2011 to 2013

Table 4.3 Gender equality and genocide

Country	Gender Equality Score	Genocide
Burundi	0.710	0
Uganda	0.707	0
Angola	0.635	0
Nigeria	0.628	1
Ethiopia	0.595	1

Table 4.4 Covariance, standard deviation of gender equality, standard deviation of genocide, and Bravais-Pearson correlation coefficient

COVARIANCE	−0.017
STANDARD DEVIATION GENDER EQUALITY	0.051
STANDARD DEVIATION GENOCIDE	0.548
BRAVAIS-PEARSON CORRELATION COEFFICIENT	−0.621

To empirically test the correlation between gender equality and genocide, I calculated the covariance, the SD for gender equality and genocide, and the Bravais-Pearson correlation coefficient (see Table 4.4).

The negative value of the *covariance* shows that between gender equality and the presence of genocide there is an inverse relation, i.e. to lower scores of gender equality there are higher possibilities of genocide; and on the contrary, in presence of higher gender equality scores the risk of genocide is lower. Similarly, the negative value of the Bravais-Pearson correlation coefficient shows that there is a negative correlation between the two variables and that when gender equality decreases, the presence of genocide increases.

To this, it adds the value of the intensity of this correlation, showing that there is a moderate correlation.[1] These data do not necessarily show a cause-effect relationship, but just the variation of one variable according to the variation of another variable. Given these results, it is possible to conclude that there is a correlation between gender equality and genocide, and in the presence of lower scores for gender equality there are higher possibilities of genocide. The research hypothesis is confirmed.

Note

1 The SD data are useful to calculate the Bravais-Pearson correlation coefficient.

5 Conclusions

It is both politically and normatively desirable to act to prevent mass atrocity crimes from being committed rather than to react after they are already underway. In fact, not only to prevent atrocities save lives, but it is also less expensive than reaction and rebuilding, and above all, it solves the dilemma between respecting State sovereignty and interference. However, it is difficult to translate rhetorical support for the prevention of genocide and mass atrocities into a cohesive strategy. For the relationship between armed conflict and mass atrocities is highly complex and yet not well understood. Atrocity prevention requires tailored engagement. In fact, not all conflicts give rise to mass atrocities and many atrocities occur in the absence of armed struggle. Therefore, it is not to assume that efforts to prevent or resolve conflict will always simultaneously reduce the likelihood of mass atrocity crimes, including genocide. Moreover, while an appreciation of particular regional and local dynamics is critical, many of the most promising preventive tools such as finding or monitoring missions, satellite surveillance, mediation, targeted sanctions, or no-fly zones require already existing structures, skills, and technology if they are to be applied in a timely and effective fashion.

Furthermore, prevention of genocide is still partial and some indicators are still missing. In fact, for as accurate they are, risk assessment and models for genocide prevention are not perfectly accurate yet. Existing early warning mechanisms to prevent mass atrocities are almost totally gender-blind, which means that they do not recognize any distinction between the sexes and incorporate biases not recognizing that women and men are constrained in different and often unequal ways by atrocities and therefore may have different needs, interests, and priorities. Conversely to this trend, many scholars have argued that a domestic environment of gender inequality and violence results in greater likelihood of violence both at national

and international levels. According to the existing literature, there is a correlation between levels of violence, international conflicts, intrastate armed
conflicts, civil war, and gender inequality. Societies that are more equitable
are supposed to be more peaceful because women have a say over matters
of war and peace (and they are generally more averse to war than men are),
and because the norms of inviolability and respect that define equal relations between women and men are carried over to wider relations in society.
This research aimed at upgrading this line of inquiry. It sought to discover
what impact gender equality has on genocide. The research hypothesis was
that the lower gender equality is, the greater the likelihood that a State will
experience genocide. The aim of this project was to test whether States characterized by lower levels of gender equality are more likely to experience
genocide. Beyond theoretical inquiry, I calculated the covariance, the standard deviation for gender equality and genocide, and the Bravais-Pearson
correlation coefficient to test the preceding hypothesis, taking Nigeria, Ethiopia, Angola, Burundi, and Uganda in 2009 as case studies. This research
analysed overall gender equality in these five countries through the data of
the Global Gender Gap Report 2009 from the World Economic Forum and
through OECD's (Organization for Economic Cooperation and Development) Social Institutions and Gender Index (SIGI). Starting from Barbara
Harff and Ted Gurr's Country Risks of Genocide and Politicide Index Score
(2009), I used gender equality to try to understand why, with similar scores,
some countries experienced genocide while others did not. The main goal
was to test whether there is a correlation between gender equality and genocide, in order to start considering the addition of gender indicators in the
genocide prevention models and early warning mechanisms concerning the
Responsibility to Protect.

   The presence/absence of genocide was tested with Genocide Alert by
Gregory Stanton's Genocide Watch. The research showed that Ethiopia
(where the genocide was already underway in 2009) got the same score (in
Harff and Gurr's Risk Index Score) as Angola where, according to Genocide Watch, the level of violence did not turn into genocidal violence, even
after 2009. Moreover, Nigeria (the only country that experienced genocide
after 2009) got the lowest score among the five case studies. Thus, to the
usual considered variables calculated in Harff and Gurr's Risk Index Score,
I added an analysis on gender equality in the case studies to measure the
'weight' that gender equality had on the eruption of genocidal violence,
using the data elaborated by the Global Gender Gap Report from the World
Economic Forum. The results showed that the two countries that experienced genocide were also the ones with lower gender equality scores. The
negative value of the covariance showed that between gender equality and
the presence of genocide there is an inverse relation, i.e. to lower scores of

gender equality there are higher possibilities of genocide; and on the contrary, in the presence of higher gender equality scores the risk of genocide is lower. Similarly, the negative value of the Bravais-Pearson correlation coefficient showed that there is a negative correlation between the two variables and that when gender equality decreases the presence of genocide increases. To this, the value of the intensity of this correlation showed that there is a moderate correlation. These results do not necessarily show a cause-effect relationship, but just the variation of one variable according to the variation of another variable. However, given these results, it is possible to conclude that there is a correlation between gender equality and genocide, and in presence of lower scores of gender equality, there are higher possibilities of genocide. The research hypothesis is confirmed. Consequently, the process of engendering early warning, by integrating a gender perspective into all stages of early warning of genocide prevention, at all levels, not confining gender issues to a single process, can improve existing approaches of information collection, analysis, and response formulation. Moreover, engendering early warning is not only beneficial for anticipating genocide early in the process of violence escalation, but it might also lead to more 'fine-tuned' policy recommendations (i.e. reducing gender inequality as a means to reduce the risk of genocide). This should lead us to consider the need to add gender indicators to the existing early warning assessment for the prevention of genocide and the need for greater commitment to improve gender equality through formulation of policies directed at improvement not just as a means to improve women's conditions, but also as a tool to reduce the risk of genocide and mass atrocities concerning the Responsibility to Protect, because the negative repercussions that gender inequality has at the societal level go beyond the negative impact on women alone.

Bibliography

ACAT and OMCT, (2008), 'Report on Violence against Women in Burundi: Executive Summary', available at www2.ohchr.org/english/bodies/cedaw/docs/ngos/acatomctburundi.pdf (viewed 13 January 2016).

Action for Development [ACFODE], (2009), 'Sexual and Gender Based Violence in Uganda: Experiences of Sexual Violence among Women and Girls in Pallisa and Kisoro Districts', Baseline Survey, available at http://menengage.org/wp-content/uploads/2014/06/Sexual_and_Gender_Based_Violence_in_Uganda1.pdf (viewed 3 April 2016).

Adelman H., (1998), 'Defining Humanitarian Early Warning', in Susanne Schmeidl and Howard Adelman (eds.), *Early Warning and Early Response*, New York: Columbia International Affairs Online (Columbia University Press).

Adler R., Fishman P., Larson E., and Smith J., (2004), 'To Prevent, React, and Rebuild: Health Research and the Prevention of Genocide', *Health Service Research* 39(6): 2027–2052.

African Development Bank, (2008), 'Annual Report 2008', available at www.afdb.org/en/knowledge/publications/annual-report/annual-report-2008/ (viewed 14 January 2016).

Agbiboa D., and Maiangwa B., (2014), 'Why Boko Haram Kidnap Girls in Nigeria', in Vasu Gounden (ed.), *Conflict Trend* (3): 51.

Ahmed A., and Kassinis E., (1998), 'The Humanitarian Early Warning System: From Concept to Practice', in John L. Davies and Ted Robert Gurr (eds.), *Preventive Measures: Building Risk Assessment and Crises Early Warning Systems*, Lanham, MD: Rowman and Littlefield Publishers.

Alemu B., and Asnake M., (2007), *Women's Empowerment in Ethiopia: New Solutions to Ancient Problems*, Ethiopia: Pathfinder International.

Amnesty International, (2007), 'Doubly Traumatised: Lack of Access to Justice for Victims of Sexual and Gender-based Violence in Northern Uganda', AI Index: AFR 59/005/2007 p. 3.

Anderlini S., (2006), 'Mainstreaming Gender in Conflict Analysis: Issues and Recommendations', Social Development Papers, no. 33, World Bank, Washington DC, available at www-wds.worldbank.org/servlet/WDSContentServer/WDSP/IB/2006/02/13/000090341_20060213143713/Rendered/PDF/351500Mainstreaming0gender0WP3301Public1.pdf (viewed 4 March 2015).

Aroussi S., (2011), 'Women, Peace and Security: Addressing Accountability for Wartime Sexual Violence', *International Feminist Journal of Politics* 13(4): 576–593.

Atama G., (2012), 'Girl-child Education: A Challenge for Sustainable Development in Nigeria', *Mediterranean Journal of Social Sciences* 3(14).

Attinà F., (2011), *The Global Political System*, Basingstoke: Palgrave Macmillan.

Baller R., Zevenbergen M., and Messner S., (2009), 'The Heritage of Herding and Southern Homicide: Examining the Ecological Foundations of the Code of Honor Thesis', *Journal of Research in Crime and Delinquency* 46: 275–300.

Ballif-Spanvill B., Caprioli M., Emmett C., and Hudson V., (2007), 'Walking a Fine Line: Addressing Issues of Gender with Woman Stats', Paper Presented at the Annual International Studies Association Conference, 28 February–3 March, Chicago, IL.

Ballif-Spanvill B., Caprioli M., Emmett C., and Hudson V., (2008), 'The Heart of the Matter: The Security of Women and the Security of States', *International Security* 33(3): 7–45.

Ballif-Spanvill B., Caprioli M., Emmett C., and Hudson V., (2012), *Sex and World Peace*, New York: Columbia University Press.

Ban Ki-moon, (2012), 'Address to the Stanley Foundation Conference on Responsibility to Protect', New York, available at www.r2p10.org (viewed 12 August 2016).

Bartelson J., (1996), 'Short-circuits: Society and Traditions in International Relations Theory', *Review of International Studies* 22: 339–360.

Bartoli A., Bauer Y., and Gurr T., (2010), 'What Is Known about Prevention and Mitigation of Genocidal Violence', Papers from the Meeting of the Genocide Prevention Advisory Network, available at www.gpanet.org/content/genocide-prevention-advisory-network-2010 (viewed 11 September 2015).

Bartrop P., (2014), *Genocide: The Basics*, New York: Routledge.

Bauer Y., (2010), 'Some Current Problems of Genocide Prevention', Published online in Prevention and Mitigation of Genocide and Mass Atrocities: Focus on East and Central Africa and the Islamic World, Genocide Prevention Advisory Network (GPA Net), p. 4.

Bazza H., (2010), 'Domestic Violence and Women's Rights in Nigeria', *Societies Without Borders* 4(2): 175–192, available at http://scholarlycommons.law.case.edu/swb/vol4/iss2/6 (viewed 23 June 2016).

BBC News, (2009), 'Uganda to Continue Congo LRA Hunt', available at http://news.bbc.co.uk/2/hi/africa/7926173.stm (viewed 8 August 2015).

BBC News, (2016a), 'Angola Country Profile', available at www.bbc.com/news/world-africa-13036732 (viewed 26 September 2015).

BBC News, (2016b), 'Burundi Country Profile', available at www.bbc.com/news/world-africa-13085064 (viewed 25 September 2015).

BBC News, (2016c), 'Ethiopia Country Profile', available at www.bbc.com/news/world-africa-13349398 (viewed 27 September 2015).

BBC News, (2016d), 'Nigeria Country Profile', available at www.bbc.co.uk/news/world-africa-13949550 (viewed 26 September 2015).

BBC News, (2016e), Uganda Country Profile', available at www.bbc.co.uk/news/world-africa-14107906 (viewed 25 September 2015).

Beck T., (1999), *Using Gender Sensitive Indicators: A Reference Manual for Governments and Other Stakeholders*, Gender Management Series, London: Commonwealth Secretariat.

Bellamy A., (2006), 'What Will Become of the "Responsibility to Protect"?' *Ethics and International Affairs* 20(2): 143–169.

Bellamy A., (2008), 'The Responsibility to Protect and the Problem of Military Intervention', *International Affairs* 84(4): 615–639.

Bellamy A., (2009), *Responsibility to Protect: The Global Effort to End Mass Atrocities*, Cambridge: Polity Press.

Bellamy A., (2010), 'The Responsibility to Protect – Five Years on', *Ethics and International Affairs* 24(2): 143–169.

Bellamy A., (2011), 'Mass Atrocities and Armed Conflict: Links, Distinctions and Implication for the Responsibility to Prevent', Policy Analysis Briefs, Innovative Approaches to Peace and Security from the Stanley Foundation, The Stanley Foundation.

Belligni S., (1991), *I Paradigmi del politico*, Torino: Giappichelli.

Bergen D., (2006), 'Religion and Genocide: A Historiographical Survey', in Dan Stone (ed.), *The Historiography of Genocide*, New York: Palgrave Macmillan.

Berhane Y., (2005), 'Ending Domestic Violence against Women in Ethiopia', *Ethiopian Journal on Health and Development* 18(3): 131–132.

Bloxham D., (2009), *The Final Solution: A Genocide*, Oxford: Oxford University Press.

Bond J., and Sherret L., (2006), 'A Sight for Sore Eyes: Bringing Gender Vision to the Responsibility to Protect Doctrine', Published online on the United Nations International Research and Training Institute for the Advancement of Women (INSTRAW).

Bond J., and Sherret L., (2012), 'Mapping Gender and the Responsibility to Protect: Seeking Intersections, Finding Parallels', *Global Responsibility to Protect* 4(2): 133–153.

Bonta B., (1996), 'Conflict Resolution among Peaceful Societies: The Culture of Peacefulness', *Journal of Peace Research* 33(4): 403–420.

Boyer M., and Caprioli M., (2001a), 'Feminist Reflections on the Responsibility to Protect', *Global Responsibility to Protect* 2(3): 232–249.

Boyer M., and Caprioli M., (2001b), 'Gender, Violence, and International Crisis', *Journal of Conflict Resolution* 45(4): 503–518.

Boyer M., Caprioli M., Denemark R., and Lamy S., (2003), 'Visions of International Studies in a New Millennium', *International Studies Perspectives* 1(1): 1–9.

Breakey H., (2011), *The Responsibility to Protect and The Protection of Civilians in Armed Conflicts: Review and Analysis*, Institute for Ethics: Governance and Law, Griffith University.

Brown R., Osterman L., and Barnes C., (2009), 'School Violence and the Culture of Honor', *Journal of Psychological Science* 20(11): 1400–1405, Sage Journals.

Brysk A., and Mehta A., (2013), 'Do Rights at Home Boost Right Abroad? Sexual Equality and Humanitarian Foreign Policy', *Journal of Peace Research* published online 29 October, Sage Publications.

Brock-Utne B., (1990), 'Feminist Perspectives on Peace', in P. Smoker, R. Davies and B. Munske (eds.), *A Reader in Peace Studies*, pp. 144–150, New York: Pergamon Press.

Buchanan A., (1999), 'The Internal Legitimacy of Humanitarian Intervention', *The Journal of Political Philosophy* 7(1): 71–87.

Buchanan A., and Keohane R., (2004), 'The Preventive Use of Force: A Cosmopolitan Institutional Proposal', *Ethics and International Affairs* 18(1): 1–22.

Bull H., (1977), *The Anarchical Society: A Study of Order in International Society*, New York: Columbia University Press.

Bunch C., and Carrillo R., (1998), 'Global Violence against Women: The Challenge to Human Rights and Development', in M. T. Klare and Y. Chandrani (eds.), *World Security*, pp. 229–248, New York, NY: St. Martin's Press.

Butcher C., Goldsmith B., Semenovich D., et al., (2012), 'Understanding and Forecasting Political Instability and Genocide for Early Warning', p. 12, available at http://sydney.edu.au/arts/research/atrocity_forecasting/downloads/docs/GenocideForecasting ReportGlobal_2012afp.pdf (viewed 9 April 2016).

Caprioli M., (1999), 'Predicting State Bellicosity: The Role of Democracy, Equality, and Economics', *Doctoral Dissertations*, Paper AAI9924295.

Caprioli M., (2000), 'Gendered Conflict', *Journal of Peace Research* 37(1): 53–68, Sage Publications.

Caprioli M., (2003), 'Gender Equality and State Aggression: The Impact of Domestic Gender Equality on State First Use of Force', *International Interactions* 29(3): 195–214.

Caprioli M., (2004a), 'Democracy and Human Rights versus Women's Security: A Contradiction?' *Security Dialogue* 35(4): 411–428.

Caprioli M., (2004c), 'Multiple Pathways to Understanding: A Response to Bilgin', *Security Dialogue* 35(4): 505–508.

Caprioli M., (2004b), 'Feminist IR Theory and Quantitative Methodology: A Critical Analysis', *International Studies Review* 6(2): 253.

Caprioli M., (2005), 'Primed for Violence: The Role of Gender Inequality in Predicting Internal Conflict', *International Studies Quarterly* 49(2): 161–178.

Caprioli M., (2007), 'Feminist Methodologies for International Relations', *Perspectives on Politics* 5(3).

Caprioli M., (2009), 'Making Choices', *Politics and Gender* 5(3): 426–431.

Caprioli M., and Douglass K., (2008), 'Nation Building and Women: The Effect of Intervention on Women's Agency', *Foreign Policy Analysis* 4(1): 45–65.

Caprioli M., McDermott R., Hudson V., and Stearmer M., (2009), 'The Woman Stats Project Database: Advancing an Empirical Research Agenda', *Journal of Peace Research* 46(5).

Caprioli M., and Trumbore P., (2003b), 'Identifying "Rogue" States and Testing Their Interstate Conflict Behavior', *European Journal of International Relations* 9(3): 377–406.

Caprioli M., and Trumbore P., (2003a), 'Ethnic Discrimination and Interstate Violence: Testing the International Impact of Domestic Behavior', *Journal of Peace Research* 40(1): 5–23.

Caprioli M., and Trumbore P., (2005), 'Rhetoric versus Reality: Rogue States in Interstate Conflict', *Journal of Conflict Resolution* 49(5): 770–791.

Caprioli M., and Trumbore P., (2006a), 'First Use of Violent Force in Militarized Interstate Disputes, 1980–2001', *Journal of Peace Research* 43(6): 741–749.

Caprioli M., and Trumbore P., (2006b), 'Human Rights Rogues in Interstate Disputes, 1980–2001', *Journal of Peace Research* 43(2).

Chalk F., and Jonassohn K., (1990), *The History and Sociology of Genocide: Analyzes and Case Studies*, New Haven and London: Yale University Press.

Charny I., (1994), 'Toward a Generic Definition of Genocide', in George J. Andreopoulos (ed.), *Genocide: Conceptual and Historical Dimensions*, pp. 64–94, Philadelphia: University of Pennsylvania Press.

Chataway T., (2007), 'Towards Normative Consensus on Responsibility to Protect', *Griffith Law Review* 16: 193–224.

Choomaraswamyn R., (2003), *Integration of the Human Rights of Women and the Gender Perspective-Violence against Women*, United Nations Economic and Social Council Commission of Human Rights, p. 134.

The Coalition Against Gender Violence and UNFPA, (2004), 'Assessment of Gender Violence in Apac and Mbale Districts of Uganda', Addis Ababa Ethiopia, p. 39.

Cockburn C., (2010), 'Gender Relations as Causal in Militarization and War', *International Feminist Journal of Politics* 12(2): 139–157.

Committee on the Elimination of All Forms of Discrimination against Women (CEDAW), (2008), 'Concluding Comments of the Committee on the Elimination of Discrimination against Women: Burundi', CEDAW/C/BDI/CO/4, Committee on the Elimination of Discrimination against Women, New York, NY.

Constitution of the Republic of Uganda, (1995), available at www.ulii.org/node/23824 (viewed 3 August 2016).

Consultoria de Serviços e Pesquisas – COSEP Lda., Consultoria de Gestão e Administração em Saúde – Consaúde Lda. [Angola], and Macro International Inc., (2007), *Angola Malaria Indicator Survey 2006–07*, Calverton, MD: COSEP Lda., Consaúde Lda., and Macro International Inc.

Dandrian V., (1975), 'A Typology of Genocide', *International Review of Sociology* 5(2): 201–212.

Das V., (2006), 'Collective Violence and the Shifting Categories of Communal Riots, Ethnic Cleansing and Genocide', in Dan Stone (ed.), *The Historiography of Genocide*, New York: Palgrave Macmillan.

Daumerie B., and Madson E., (2010), *The Effects if a Very Young Structure in Uganda: The Shape of Things to Come Series*, Washington, DC: Population Action International.

Davis S., Nkokora Z., and Teitt S., (2015), 'Bridging the Gap: Early Warning, Gender and the Responsibility to Protect', *Cooperation and Conflict* 50(2): 228–249.

Davis S., and Teitt S., (2012), 'Engendering the Responsibility to Protect: Women and the Prevention of Mass Atrocities', *Global Responsibility to Protect* 4(2): 198–222.

Dedring J., (1994), 'Early Warning and the United Nations', *The Journal of Ethno-Development: Special Issue on Early Warning of Communal Conflicts and Humanitarian* Crises 4(1): 98–105.

Deng F., Rothchild P., and Zartmann W., (1996), *Sovereignty as Responsibility: Conflict Management in Africa*, Washington, DC: Brookings Institution.

Diamond L., (1987), 'Muslim Hausa Women in Nigeria: Tradition and Change', *The Journal of Modern African Studies* 25(4): 692–694.

Dietz M., (1985), 'Citizenship with a Feminist Face: The Problem with Maternal Thinking', *Political Theory* 13: 19–35.

Ducados H., (2004), 'Angolan Women in the Aftermath of Conflict', available at www.c-r.org/our-work/accord/angola/women-conflict.php (viewed 12 February 2016).

El-Bushra J., and Sahl I., (2005), 'Cycles of Violence Gender Relations and Armed Conflict', available at www.acordinternational.org/silo/files/cycles-of-violence-gender-relationa-and-armed-conflict.pdf (viewed 14 January 2016).

Ekval A., (2000), 'Gender Equality, Attitudes to Gender Equality and Conflict', in Marcia Texler Segal and Vasilikie Demos (eds.), *Gendered Perspectives on Conflict and Violence: Advances in Gender Research*, Volume 18, pp. 273–295, Bingley: Emerald Group Publishing Limited.

Esteve-Volart B., (2000), 'Sex Discrimination and Growth', IMF Working Paper No. 00/84, available at SSRN: https://ssrn.com/abstract=879613 (viewed 11 May 2016).

Evans G., (2006), 'From Humanitarian Intervention to the Responsibility to Protect', *Wisconsin International Law Journal* 24(3): 703–722.

Ezeliora B., (2005), 'Emerging Trend in Male and Female Undergraduate Enrolment into Universities. A Case Study of South East Zone of Nigeria', A Paper Presented at International Conference of Transatlantic Research Group in Association with Echeruo Centre for Public Policy.

Ezeliora B., and Ezeokana J., (2011), 'Inhibiting Influences of Some Traditional Practices in the Home on Girl-child's Interest Development in Science', *African Journal of Political Sciences and International Relations* 5(7): 341–346.

Feierstein D., (2007), *El genocidio como practica social: entre en nazismo y la experiencia Argentina*, Buenos Aires: Fondo de Cultura Economica.

Fein H., (1993), *Genocide: A Sociological Perspective*, Newbury Park: Sage Publications.

FEWER, (1999), *FEWER Conflict and Peace Analysis and Response Manual*, London: FEWER.

Fish M., (2002), 'Islam and Authoritarianism', *World Politics* 55: 4–37.

Fourth World Conference on Women, (1995), 'Beijing Declaration and Platform for Action', available at www.unwomen.org/~/media/headquarters/attachments/sections/csw/pfa_e_final_web.pdf (viewed 27 July 2015).

Francis D., (2004), 'Culture, Power Asymmetries and Gender in Conflict Transformation', in *Berghof Handbook for Conflict Transformation*, Berghof: Berghof Research Centre for Constructive Conflict Management.

Freedom House, (2009a), 'Freedom in the World Annual Report – Angola Country Profile', available at https://freedomhouse.org/report/freedom-world/2009/angola (viewed 8 March 2016).

Freedom House (2009b), 'Freedom in the World Annual Report – Burundi Country Profile', available at https://freedomhouse.org/report/freedom-world/2009/burundi (viewed 9 August 2015).

Freedom House, (2009c), 'Freedom in the World Annual Report – Ethiopia Country Profile', available at https://freedomhouse.org/report/freedom-world/2009/ethiopia (viewed 17 December 2015).

Freedom House, (2009d), 'Freedom in the World Annual Report – Nigeria Country Profile', available at https://freedomhouse.org/report/freedom-world/2009/nigeria (viewed 6 September 2014).

Freedom House, (2009e), 'Freedom in the World Annual Report – Uganda Country Profile', available at https://freedomhouse.org/report/freedom-world/2009/uganda (viewed 15 December 2015).

Galtung J., (1975), 'Peace: Research, Education, Action', in *Essay in Peace Research Volume One*. Bucuresti, Romania: CIPEXIM.

Galtung J., (1993), 'Kulturell Gewalt', *Der Burger im Staat* 43: 106.

Geneva Declaration on Armed Violence and Development, (2011), 'Global Burden of Armed Violence 2011', available at www.genevadeclaration.org/en/measurability/global-burden-of-armed-violence/global-burden-of-armed-violence-2011.html (viewed 13 October 2016).

Genocide Watch, (1999), 'Genocide Watch', available at http://genocidewatch.net (viewed 3 June 2014).

Genocide Watch, (2012a), 'Angola Country Profile', available at http://genocidewatch.net/2012/12/07/country-profile-angola/ (viewed 2 September 2015).

Genocide Watch, (2012b), 'Burundi Country Profile', available at http://genocidewatch.net/2012/11/01/country-profile-burundi/ (viewed 4 September 2015).

Genocide Watch, (2012c), 'Ethiopia Country Profile', available at http://genocidewatch.net/2012/12/06/country-profile-ethiopia-2/ (viewed 14 July 2015).

Genocide Watch, (2012d), 'Genocide Watch Alert: Ethiopia', available at http://genocidewatch.net/2012/12/06/genocide-watch-emergency-ethiopia/ (viewed 24 March 2015).

Genocide Watch, (2012e), 'Genocide Watch Emergency Alert: Ethiopia', available at http://genocidewatch.net/2012/12/06/genocide-watch-emergency-ethiopia/ (viewed 24 March 2015).

Genocide Watch, (2012f), 'Genocide Watch Emergency Update: Ethiopia', available at http://genocidewatch.net/2012/12/06/genocide-watch-emergency-ethiopia/ (viewed 24 March 2015).

Genocide Watch, (2012g), 'Nigeria Country Profile', available at http://genocidewatch.net/2012/12/07/country-profile-nigeria/ (viewed 15 December 2014).

Genocide Watch, (2012h), 'Uganda Country Profile', available at http://genocidewatch.net/2012/12/06/country-profile-uganda/ (viewed 4 March 2016).

Genocide Watch, (2013), 'Ten Stages of Genocide', available at http://genocidewatch.net/genocide-2/8-stages-of-genocide/ (viewed 6 November 2014).

Genocide Watch, (2014), 'Genocide Watch Emergency Alert: Nigeria', available at http://genocidewatch.net/2014/09/04/nigeria-genocide-emergency-alert/ (viewed 5 November 2014).

Genocide Watch, (2015), 'Genocide Watch Alert: Burundi', available at http://genocidewatch.net/2015/08/11/genocide-watch-alert-2015-on-burundi/ (viewed 3 March 2015).

Goldstein J., (2001), *War and Gender: How Gender Shapes the War System and Vice Versa*, Cambridge: Cambridge University Press.

Gordenker L., (1992), 'Early Warning: Conceptual and Practical Issues', in Kumar Rupesinghe and Michiko Kuroda (eds.), *Early Warning and Conflict Resolution*. London: Palgrave Macmillan.

Gurr T., (1996), 'Early Warning Systems: From Surveillance to Assessment of Action', in Kevin M. Chill (ed.), *Preventive Diplomacy: Stopping Wars Before They Start*, pp. 123–144, New York: Basic Books.

Gurr T., (2010), 'East and Central Africa: A Legacy of Deadly Political Violence and the Risks of Its Recurrence', Published online in Prevention and Mitigation of Genocide and Mass Atrocities: Focus on East and Central Africa and the Islamic World, Genocide Prevention Advisory Network (GPA Net), p. 7.

Harff B., (1998), 'Early Warning of Humanitarian Crises: Sequential Models and the Role of Accelerators', in John L. Davies and Ted Robert Gurr (eds.), *Preventive Measures: Building Risk Assessment and Crises Early Warning Systems*, Lanham, MD: Rowman and Littlefield Publishers.

Harff B., (2003), 'No Lessons Learned from the Holocaust? Assessing Risks of Genocide and Political Mass Murder since 1955', *American Political Science Review* 57–73.

Harff B., (2012), 'Assessing Risks of Genocide and Politicide: A Global Watch List for 2012', in Birger Heldt (ed.), *Peace and Conflict 2012*, p. 21, Center for International Development and Conflict Management–University of Maryland.

Harff B., and Gurr T., (2009), 'Assessing Country Risks of Genocide and Politicide in 2009', available at www.gpanet.org/ (viewed 14 December 2014).

Hewitt J., (2009), 'The Peace and Conflict Instability Ledger: Ranking States on Future Risks', in J. Joseph Hewitt, Jonathan Wilkenfeld, and T. R Gurr (eds.), *Peace and Conflict 2010*, pp. 7–26, Boulder, CO: Paradigm Publishers.

Herbert S., (2014), *Links Between Gender Based Violence and Outbreaks of Violent Conflict*, GSDRC Helpdesk report. Birmingham, UK: GSDRC, University of Birmingham.

Hill F., (2003), 'The Elusive Role of Women in Early Warning and Conflict Prevention', *Conflict Trends* 3: 11–17.

Horowitz I., (1976), *Genocide: State Power & Mass Murder*, New Brunswick, NJ: Transaction Books.

Huising F., (2013), 'A Responsibility to Prevent? A Norm's Political and Legal Effects', *Amsterdam Law Forum* 5(1): 4–35.

Hulsizer L., and Woolf M., (2005), 'Psychosocial Roots of Genocide: Risk, Prevention, and Intervention', *Journal of Genocide Research* 7(1): 101–128, Routledge Taylor and Francis Group.

Human Rights Watch, (2007), 'Angola', available at www.unhcr.org/cgibin/texis/vtx/refworld/rwmain?page=printdoc&docid=45aca29816 (viewed 3 February 2016).

Inglis T., and MacKeogh C., (2012), 'The Double Bind: Women, Honour and Sexuality in Contemporary Ireland', *Media Culture & Society* 34(1): 68–82.

International Commission on Intervention and State Sovereignty, Report on the Responsibility to Protect, (December 2001), available at http://responsibility toprotect.org/ICISS%20Report.pdf (viewed 19 May 2015).

Ijzerman H., and Cohen D., (2011), 'Grounding Cultural Syndromes: Body Comportment and Values in Honor and Dignity Cultures', *European Journal of Social Psychology* 41(4): 456–467.

Institute on the Holocaust and Genocide Jerusalem, (1999), *Encyclopedia of Genocide*, ed. Israel Charny, Santa Barbara, CA: ABC Clio.

Jekayinfa A., (2007), 'The Status of Female Citizens in the Nigerian Socio-cultural Environments: Implications for Social Studies Education', *Nigerian Journal of Social Studies* X(1–2): 241–252.

Jones A., (2006), *Genocide: A Comprehensive Introduction*, New York: Routledge.

Kasin–Oghabor F., (2005), 'Culture as Constraint in Women Education: A Study of Ukwuani in Delta State', *International Journal of Forum for African Women Educationist* 1(1): 42–48.

Katz S., (1994), *The Holocaust in Historical Context*, Volume 1, Oxford: Oxford University Press.

King E., and Mason A., (2001), *Engendering Development: Through Gender Equality in Rights, Resources and Voice*, Washington, DC and New York: The World Bank and Oxford University Press. A World Bank Policy Research Report.

Kressel N., (1996), *Mass Hate: The Global Rise of Genocide and Terror*, New York: Plenum Press.

Korteweg C., and Yurdakul G., (2010), 'Religion, Culture and the Politicization of Honour-Related Violence a Critical Analysis of Media and Policy Debates in Western Europe and North America', *Gender and Development*. Programme Paper Number 12. United Nations. Research Institute for Social Development.

Kuhn T., (1962), *The Structure of Scientific Revolutions*, Chicago: University of Chicago Press.

Kuper L., (1981), *Genocide: Its Political Use in the Twentieth Century*, New Haven, CT: Yale University Press.

Lemkin R., (1944), *Axis Rule in Occupied Europe: Laws of Occupation, Analysis of Government, Proposals for Redress*, Washington, DC: Carnegie Endowment for International Peace, Division of International Law.

Leonhardt C., (2000), *Conflict Impact Assessment of EU Development Cooperation with ACP Countries: A Review of Literature and Practice*, London: International Alert, Saferworld.

Lyons M., and Mastanduno M., (1995), *Beyond Westphalia? State Sovereignty and International Intervention*, Baltimore: John Hopkins University Press.

Luck E., (2009), 'Sovereignty, Choice, and the Responsibility to Protect', *Global Responsibility to Protect* 1: 10–21.

Marshall M., and Cole B., (2009), 'Global Report 2009: Conflict, Governance, and State Fragility', Center for Systemic Peace and George Mason University's Center for Global Policy, available at www.systemicpeace.org (viewed 14 April 2015).

Marshall M., and Ramsey D., (1999), 'Gender Empowerment and the Willingness to Use Force', Paper Presented at the Annual Convention of the International Studies Association Annual Meeting, Washington, DC, 16–20 February.

Maoz Z., (2003), 'The Controversy over the Democratic Peace: Rearguard Action or Cracks in the Wall?' *International Security* 22(1): 162–198.

Matveeva A., (2006), 'Early Warning and Early Response: Conceptual and Empirical Dilemmas', available at www.peaceportal.org/documents/127900679/127917167/Issue+paper+1-+Early+Warning+and+Early+Response.pdf (viewed 28 September 2018).

Melander E., (2005a), 'Gender Equality and Intrastate Armed Conflict', *International Studies Quarterly* 49: 695–714.

Melander E., (2005b), 'Political Gender Equality and State Human Rights Abuse', *Journal of Peace Research* 42(2): 149–166, Sage Publications.

Moser C., (2001), 'The Gendered Continuum of Violence and Conflict: An Operational Framework', in C. Moser and F. Clare (eds.), *Victims, Perpetrators or Actors: Gender, Armed Conflict and Political Violence*, p. 43, London: Zed Press.

Moser A., (2007), 'Gender and Indicators: Overview Report', Report, UNDP and Institute for Development Studies, New York, July.

Naimark N., (2001), *Fires of Hatred: Ethnic Cleansing in Twentieth Century Europe*, Cambridge: Harvard University Press.

National Population Commission (NPC) [Nigeria] and ICF Macro, (2009), *Nigeria Demographic and Health Survey 2008*, Abuja, Nigeria: National Population Commission and ICF Macro.

Okeke J., (2008), 'The Limit of the "Responsibility to Protect" Principle in Darfur', Paper Presented at the 2008 International Studies Association Conference, San Francisco.

Organization for Economic Cooperation and Development [OECD], (2014a), 'Social Institutions and Gender Index (SIGI) – Angola Country Profile', available at www.genderindex.org/country/angola (viewed 4 May 2015).

Organization for Economic Cooperation and Development [OECD], (2009), 'Social Institutions and Gender Index (SIGI)', available at www.genderindex.org/content/team (viewed 5 July 2015).

Organization for Economic Cooperation and Development [OECD], (2014b), 'Social Institutions and Gender Index (SIGI) – Burundi Country Profile', available at www.genderindex.org/country/burundi (viewed 4 May 2015).

Organization for Economic Cooperation and Development [OECD], (2014c), 'Social Institutions and Gender Index (SIGI) – Ethiopia Country Profile', available at www.genderindex.org/country/ethiopia (viewed 4 May 2015).

Organization for Economic Cooperation and Development [OECD], (2014d), 'Social Institutions and Gender Index (SIGI) – Nigeria Country Profile', available at www.genderindex.org/country/nigeria (viewed 4 May 2015).

Organization for Economic Cooperation and Development [OECD], (2014e), 'Social Institutions and Gender Index (SIGI) – Uganda Country Profile', available at www.genderindex.org/country/uganda (viewed 4 May 2015).

Palermo T., and Peterman A., (2011), 'Undercounting, Overcounting, and the Longevity of Flawed Estimates: Statistics on Sexual Violence in Conflict', *Bulletin of the World Health Organization* 89(12): 924–925.

Pateman C., (1970), *Participation and Democratic Theory*, Cambridge, UK: Cambridge University Press.

Pattison J., (2008), 'Whose Responsibility to Protect? The Duties of Humanitarian Intervention', *Journal of Military Ethics* 7(4): 262–283.

Pattison J., (2010), *Humanitarian Intervention and the Responsibility to Protect: Who Should Intervene?* New York: Oxford University Press.

Piza-Lopez E., and Schmeild S., (2002), *Gender and Conflict Early Warning: A Preliminary Framework*, Geneva: Swiss Peace Foundation with International Alert.

PIOOM, (1999), *World Conflict and Human Rights Map*, Leiden: University of Leiden, PIOOM.

Redvers L., (2009), 'ANGOLA: Teenage School Programme Gives Drop Outs Second Chance at Education', Inter Press Service, available at www.ipsnews. net/2009/08/angola-teenage-school-programme-gives-drop-outs-second-chance-at-education/ (viewed 4 March 2016).

Report of the High Level Independent Panel on UN Peace Operation, (2015), available at https://peaceoperationsreview.org/wpcontent/uploads/2015/08/HIPPO_ Report_1_June_2015.pdf (viewed 28 September 2018).

The Republic of Uganda Ministry of Health, International Rescue Committee, UNIFEM, UNFPA, United Nations Food Programme and World Health Organization, (2005), 'Health and Mortality Survey among Internally Displaced Persons in Gulu, Kitgum and Pader Districts, Northern Uganda', available at www.who. int/hac/crises/uga/sitreps/Ugandamortsurvey.pdf (viewed 2 March 2016).

Rowbotham S., (1983), *Dreams and Dilemmas*, London: Virago Press.

Rosensaft M., (1977), 'The Holocaust: History as Aberration', *Midstream* 28(5): 55.

Rubenstein R., (1983), *The Age of Triage: Fear and Hope in an Overcrowded World*, Boston, MA: Beacon Press.

Rummel R., (1996), 'The Holocaust in Comparative and Historical Perspective', in Albert J. Jongman (ed.), *Contemporary Genocides: Causes, Cases, Consequences*, Leiden: PIOOM.

Rusu S., (1997), 'Early Warning and Information: The Role of Relief Web', in Susanne Schmeidl and Howard Adelman (eds.), *Synergy Early Warning Conference Proceedings*, York and Toronto: York University, York Center for International and Security Studies.

Saferworld, (2014), 'Gender and Conflict Early Warning: Results of a Literature Review on Integrating Gender Perspectives into Conflict Early Warning Systems', Briefing Note, available at www.saferworld.org.uk/downloads/pubdocs/ gender-and-conflict-early-warning.pdf (viewed 17 January 2016).

Saferworld & Conciliation Resources, (2014), 'Gender, Violence and Peace: A Post-2015 Development Agenda', London: Conciliation Resources, available at www.c-r.org/sites/c-r.org/files/592%20CR-Saferworld%2012page%20Draft%20 06%20pdf%20version.pdf (viewed 13 January 2016).

Schmeidl S., and Jenkins J., (1998), 'The Early Warning of Humanitarian Disasters: Problems in Building an Early Warning System', *International Migration Review* 32(2): 471–487.

Semahegn A., and Mengiste B., (2015), 'Domestic Violence against Women and Associated Factors in Ethiopia: Systematic Review', *Reproductive Health* 12: 78.

Shaw M., (2007), *What Is Genocide?* Cambridge: Polity Press, pp. 48–62.

Shija M., (2004), 'Domestic Violence and Its Impact on Women's Rights', Paper Presented at a Consultative Forum of Stakeholders to Discuss the Domestic Violence Draft Bill in Benue State, Nigeria.

Sideris T., (2001), 'Rape in War and Peace: Social Context, Gender, Power, and Identity', in S. Meintjes, A. Pillay and M. Tursher (eds.), *In the Aftermath: Women in Post-Conflict Transformation*, pp. 142–158. London: Zed Books Ltd.

Smith R., (1999), 'State Power and Genocidal Intent: On the Uses of Genocide in the Twentieth Century', in L. Chorbajian and G. Shirinian (eds.), *Studies in Comparative Genocide*, Basingstoke and New York: Palgrave Macmillan and St. Martin's Press.

Sobek D., Abouharb M., and Ingram C., (2006), 'The Human Rights Peace: How the Respect for Human Rights at Home Leads to Peace Abroad', *Journal of Politics* 68: 519–529.

Stamnes E., (2012), 'The Responsibility to Protect: Integrating Gender Perspectives into Policies and Practices', *Global Responsibility to Protect* 4(2): 173–197.

Stanton G., (1996), 'The Eight Stages of Genocide', in Totten and Bartrop (eds.), *The Genocide Studies Reader*, 127–129.

Staub E., (1999), 'The Origins and Prevention of Genocide, Mass Killings, and Other Collective Violence', *Journal of Peace Psychology* 5(4): 303–336, Lawrence Erlbaum Associates, Inc.

Tadiwos S., (2001), 'Rape in Ethiopia', Excerpts from *Reflections: Documentation of the Forum on Gender*, Panos Ethiopia, Heinrich Boell Foundation.

Tickner J., (1999), 'Why Women Can't Run the World: International Politics According to Francis Fukuyama', *International Studies Review* 1(3): 3–13.

Thompson M., (2006), 'Women, Gender, and Conflict: Making the Connections', *Development in Practice* 16(3–4) (June): 342–353, 344.

Uganda Bureau of Statistics Educational Sector, (2012), 'Gender Statistics Profile', available at www.ubos.org/onlinefiles/uploads/ubos/gender/Education%20 Sector%20Gender%20Statistics%20Profile.pdf (viewed 4 April 2016).

Ulfelder J., (2011), 'Making Case for (Imperfect) Statistical Modelling as the Basis for Genocide Early Warning', available at www.ushmm.org/genocide/analysis/ details/2011-10-05/Jay%20Ulfelder%20Early%20Warning%20Final%20Paper. pdf (viewed 9 April 2015).

United Nations, Charter of the United Nations, (1945), '1 UNTS XVI', available at www.un.org/en/charter-united-nations/ (viewed 15 July 2016).

United Nations General Assembly, Convention on the Prevention and Punishment of the Crime of Genocide, (1948), available at www.oas.org/dil/1948_Convention_on_the_Prevention_and_Punishment_of_the_Crime_of_Genocide.pdf (viewed 12 January 2015).

United Nations General Assembly, (1979), 'Convention on the Elimination of All Forms of Discrimination against Women', available at www.ohchr.org/Documents/ProfessionalInterest/cedaw.pdf (viewed 12 August 2015).

United Nations General Assembly, Rome Statute of the International Criminal Court, (1998), available at www.refworld.org/docid/3ae6b3a84.html (viewed 13 October 2016).

United Nations Women, (2000), 'Women and Armed Conflict', available at www.un.org/womenwatch/daw/followup/session/presskit/fs5.htm, (viewed 13 February 2015).

United Nations Population Fund, (2005), 'Frequently Asked Questions about Gender Equality', available at www.unfpa.org/resources/frequently-asked-questions-about-gender-equality (viewed 2 February 2015).

United Nations Secretary General, (2009), 'Implementing the Responsibility to Protect', Report of the Secretary-General, A/63/677, 12 January.

United Nations Economic Commission for Africa-African Centre for Gender and Social Development [ACGSD], (2010), 'Violence against Women in Africa: A Situational Analysis', available at www1.uneca.org/Portals/awro/Publications/21VAW% 20in%20Africa-A%20situational%20analysis.pdf (viewed 15 March 2016).

100   *Bibliography*

UN Secretary-General, (2010), 'Report of the Secretary-General: Early Warning, Assessment and the Responsibility to Protect', A/64/864, 14 July.

United Nations Secretary General, (2010), 'Report of the Secretary-General on Women, Peace and Security', S/2010/498, 26 October.

United Nations Educational, Scientific, and Cultural Organization Global Partnership for Girls' and Women's Education – One Year On, (2011), 'Girls' Education in Ethiopia', available at www.unesco.org/eri/cp/factsheets_ed/ET_EDFactSheet. pdf (viewed 23 January 2016).

United Nations Secretary General, (2011), 'Report of the Secretary General on Women and Peace Security', S/2011/598, 29 September.

United Nations Security Council, (2012), 'Cross-Cutting Report No 1 on Women Peace and Security', 27 January.

United Nations Secretary General, (2013), 'Sexual Violence in Conflict', Report of the Secretary General, S/2013/149, 14 March.

United Nations Women, (2014), 'Gender-Responsive Early Warning: Overview and User Guide', available at www.unwomen.org/~/media/Headquarters/Media/ Publications/en/04EGenderResponsiveEarlyWarning.pdf (viewed 19 April 2015).

United Nations Security Council, (2015), 'Conflict Related Sexual Violence', available at www.securitycouncilreport.org/atf/cf/%7B65BFCF9B-6D27-4E9C-8CD3-CF6E4FF96FF9%7D/s_2015_203.pdf (viewed 27 July 2015).

Urban Walker M., (2009), 'Gender and Violence in Focus', in Ruth Rubio (ed.), *Gender of Reparations: Unsettling Sexual Hierarchies while Redressing Human Right Violations*, Cambridge: Cambridge University Press.

U. S. Agency for International Development, (2006), 'Uganda – Complex Emergency', Situational Report, Bureau for Democracy, Conflict and Humanitarian Assistance [DCHA] Office of US Foreign Disaster Assistance [OFDA].

U.S. Department of State, (2008), 'Trafficking in Persons Report 2008', available at www.state.gov/j/tip/rls/tiprpt/2008/105389.htm (viewed 28 September 2018).

von Joeden-Forgey E., (2012), 'Gender and the Future of Genocide Studies and Prevention', *Genocide Studies and Prevention* 7: 89–107.

Wallimann I., and Dobkwoski M., (1987), *Genocide and the Modern Age: Etiology and Case Studies of Mass Death*, Syracuse: Syracuse University SURFACE.

Watts C., and Zimmerman C., (2002), 'Violence against Women: Global Scope and Magnitude', *The Lancet* 359(9313): 1232–1237.

Welsh J., and Sharma S., (2013), *Operationalizing the Responsibility to Prevent Secretary General Stresses Global Responsibility to Prevent Genocide*, Oxford: Oxford Institute for Ethics, Law and Armed Conflict, University of Oxford.

Wiesel E., (1976), 'Now We Know', in Richard Arens (ed.), *Genocide in Paraguay*, p. 165, Philadelphia: Temple University Press.

Woocher L., (2006), 'Developing a Strategy, Methods and Tools for Genocide Early Warning', Report Prepared for Office of the Special Advisor to the UN Secretary-General on the Prevention of Genocide, 22 September, available at www.un.org/ en/preventgenocide/adviser/pdf/Woocher%20Early%20warning%20report,%20 2006-11-10.pdf (viewed 9 April 2016).

Woodrow Wilson International Center for Scholars and Women Waging Peace, (2012), 'More Than Victims: The Role of Women in Conflict Prevention', Conference Report in Anita Wright and Lisa Freeman (eds.).

World Economic Forum, (2006), 'Global Gender Gap Report', available at www3.weforum.org/docs/WEF_GenderGap_Report_2006.pdf (viewed 14 September 2014).

Woroniuk B., (1999), 'Mainstreaming a Gender Perspective', Paper Prepared for the Canadian International Development Agency (CIDA). Ottawa, Canada: CIDA.

Zicherman N., (2007), 'Addressing Sexual Violence in Post-conflict Burundi', available at www.fmreview.org/FMRpdfs/FMR27/32.pdf (viewed 17 June 2016).

Index